Money for Life

Praise for *Money for Life*

"Today's retirees and pre-retirees face multiple challenges, including low interest rates, volatile equity markets, and the logistical headaches of turning an investment portfolio into a stream of income that will last for the rest of their lives. *Money for Life* confronts those challenges head-on, using clear examples and straightforward language to coach retirees and pre-retirees on generating the income they need without taking extreme risks. It's a valuable bookshelf addition for retirees seeking guidance on crafting a financial plan they can live with for many years."

– **Christine Benz**, director of personal finance, Morningstar, and author of *30-Minute Money Solutions: A Step-by-Step Guide to Managing Your Finances*

"This is a great book. As an actuary, I have been very concerned that many people do not understand the importance of regular lifetime income, the risk of running out of money, and the options for creating lifetime income. The decision involves trade-offs, long-term issues, and working with a range of solutions that are not easy for the average person to understand or implement. Steve Vernon has done a wonderful job of explaining the options, providing information on implementation, and cautioning about more expensive options."

– **Anna M. Rappaport**, F.S.A., M.A.A.A., chair, Society of Actuaries Committee on Post-Retirement Needs and Risks, and past president, Society of Actuaries

"Steve Vernon's book asks and answers three critical questions: When can I retire? How much do I need? How do I make it last for my lifetime . . . 20 years, 30 years or more? The book is easy to read and practical. And, importantly, Steve has the experience to be authoritative . . . and brings an unbiased, problem-solving approach to the reader."

– **Fred Reish**, partner at Drinker Biddle & Reath, chair of their ERISA Team for the Financial Services Industry

Praise for *Money for Life*

"As defined contribution plans and IRAs become an increasingly important part of retirement wealth in this country, it is essential that today's workers understand the various techniques available to convert the account balances to retirement income. Steve Vernon has done a magnificent job of drawing together in one authoritative source the benefits and potential limitations of the various strategies that should be considered by individuals."

– **Jack VanDerhei**, research director, Employee Benefit Research Institute, and editor, *Benefits Quarterly*

"How will you pay your bills in retirement – especially if you live a long, healthy life? Steve Vernon's amazing *Money for Life* provides the answers you need. Steve shares a lifetime of financial expertise in plain, easy-to-read English. Learn how to build your RIGs (retirement income generators) to last, and never worry again about out-living your money. Anyone wondering how to convert a retirement nest egg into a lifetime stream of paychecks needs this book!"

– **Andy Landis**, author of *Social Security: The Inside Story* and *When I Retire*

"*Money for Life* is an excellent primer to help you prepare a well-thought-out retirement plan. Steve Vernon touches all the right bases, making sure that you ask the right questions, including: How much money do you need in retirement? How can you generate reliable income from your retirement savings that lasts for the rest of your life? When should you retire? He not only asks the questions, he teaches you how to find the best solutions, given your own unique situation."

– **Larry Swedroe,** principal and director of research for the Buckingham Family of Financial Services, and author of *Investment Mistakes Even Smart People Make and How to Avoid Them*

Praise for *Money for Life*

"Money for Life is for retirees and pre-retirees who have a real danger of running out of money in retirement. Steve's approach addresses the insufficiency of using only a systematic withdrawal method for people with average retirement savings, where managing for retirement-specific risks must take precedence over investing strategy. Thank you for providing this actionable approach to help people make informed retirement income decisions!"

– **Betty Meredith**, CFA®, CFP®, CRC®,
International Retirement Resource Center

"Steve Vernon's *Money for Life* is a terrific resource for those of us who are looking for information and guidance to help us manage our 401(k) and IRA money to last for the next twenty or thirty years. Vernon, an actuary, provides a step-by-step retirement strategy to help figure it out. Women, in particular, need to pay close attention to *Money for Life* as they are most vulnerable to longevity risks and running out of money."

– **Cindy Hounsell**, president, Women's Institute for a Secure Retirement (WISER)

"Money for Life is consumer-focused and deserves to be widely read. It provides a balanced discussion of systematic withdrawals, annuities, or some combination, without a sales pitch for either approach."

– **Francois Gadenne**, chairman and executive director,
Retirement Income Industry Association (RIIA)

Money for Life

Turn Your IRA and 401(k) Into a Lifetime Retirement Paycheck

STEVE VERNON, FSA

Rest-of-Life Communications

Oxnard, California

Also by Steve Vernon

Recession-Proof Your Retirement Years:
Simple Retirement Planning Strategies That Work Through Thick or Thin

The Quest: For Long Life, Health and Prosperity (DVD/workbook set)

Live Long and Prosper!
Invest In Your Happiness, Health and Wealth for Retirement and Beyond

Don't Work Forever! Simple Steps Baby Boomers Must Take to Ever Retire

For bulk purchases of *Money for Life, Recession-Proof Your Retirement Years, or The Quest* DVD, please email **steve.vernon@restoflife.com**.

to Melinda
my wife and sweetie

For more information about *Rest-of-Life* Communications, visit www.restoflife.com.

Library of Congress Cataloging-in-Publication Data:

Vernon, Steven G., 1953 –
Money for Life: Turn Your IRA and 401(k) Into a Lifetime Retirement Paycheck / Steve Vernon

ISBN 978-0-9853846-0-9

1. Retirement income–United States–Planning. 2. Investments–United States. 3. Retirees–United States–Finance. 3. 401(k) –United States. 4. 401(k) –United States. I. Title

Library of Congress Control Number: 2012916226

Printed in the United States of America

TABLE OF CONTENTS

.....

Introduction

If you're like most people who are approaching retirement, you've thought long and hard about the answers to these two questions:

How much money do you need to retire?

How can you generate reliable income from your retirement savings that lasts for the rest of your life, no matter how long you live and no matter what happens in the economy?

These are critical questions for most boomers who are planning for a retirement that could easily last 20 years or more. And that leads us to the most important question of all:

When exactly can you retire?

These three questions have become particularly significant as companies continue to abandon traditional pension plans, plans in which your employer takes responsibility for funding and paying you a monthly retirement income for the rest of your life. Without these safety nets in place, planning for retirement now falls heavily on the shoulders of employees everywhere.

With the demise of pension plans, as an employee, you're now much more likely to participate in account-based plans, such as a 401(k), 403(b), 457, profit-sharing, or cash balance plan. You might also have substantial savings in an IRA or regular investment accounts. And some of you might elect a lump sum from a traditional pension plan, in which case you face the same challenges.

With these types of programs, however, you're on your own when it comes to making your money last for the rest of your life. And when your money is exhausted, there'll be nobody there to bail you out, unless you have very generous relatives or friends.

So just how much money *do* you need and how can you make it last? And when will you have enough to retire? While you could just guess, as many people do, this book will show you better ways to determine the answers to these questions.

A tale of two retirees

Here are two stories about people I know who have had to manage their own retirement savings. These stories contrast the potential outcomes of this challenge and offer important insights about the strategies that will help you achieve your retirement goals.

The first story is about a friend of mine who was a vice president of finance for a Fortune 1000 company. In 1999, he retired at age 65 with a lump sum settlement from his employer's retirement plan. At the time, the amount he received seemed like a lot of money, so he didn't change his spending habits. He simply withdrew the amounts he needed for his living expenses. He enjoyed his first years of retirement, feeling carefree, spending time with his grandkids, and doing what he'd always wanted to do, although nothing extravagant.

Unfortunately, that carefree time didn't last too long. My friend had invested substantial sums in the stock market, and two stock market crashes later, he'd exhausted his savings just 10 years after retirement. To make matters worse, he lost his home when he could no longer make the mortgage payments. He's now in his late 70s and is driving deliveries to make ends meet. His "golden years" have rusted out!

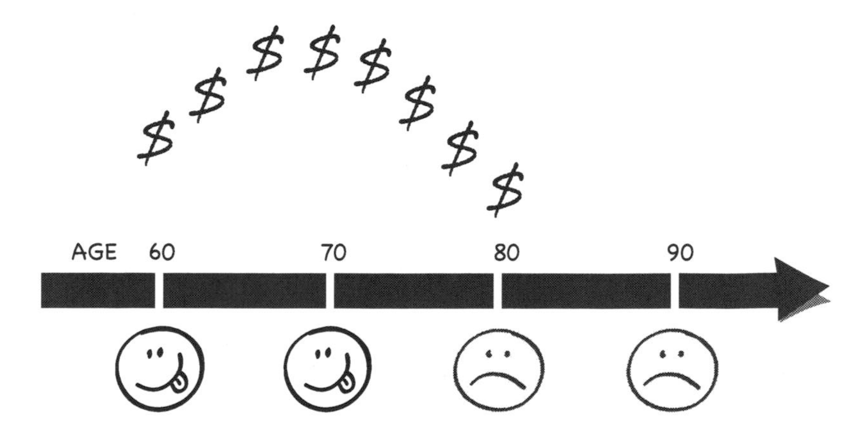

The second story concerns my 91-year-old mother. Her retirement is funded by a monthly lifetime annuity she got as a result of my father's employment as a professor at USC (my father passed away in 2005). She supplements that annuity and her Social Security income with interest and dividends earned from a carefully saved portfolio that's invested in stocks and bonds (401(k) plans didn't exist in her day). She never taps into the principal of this portfolio for day-to-day expenses; instead, it serves as a reserve in the event of financial emergencies or if she needs long-term care somewhere down the line. If the portfolio doesn't get completely depleted during her lifetime, any remaining money will pass to her heirs. With these financial plans in place, my mother has enjoyed a 31-year retirement – and counting – and she's still going strong.

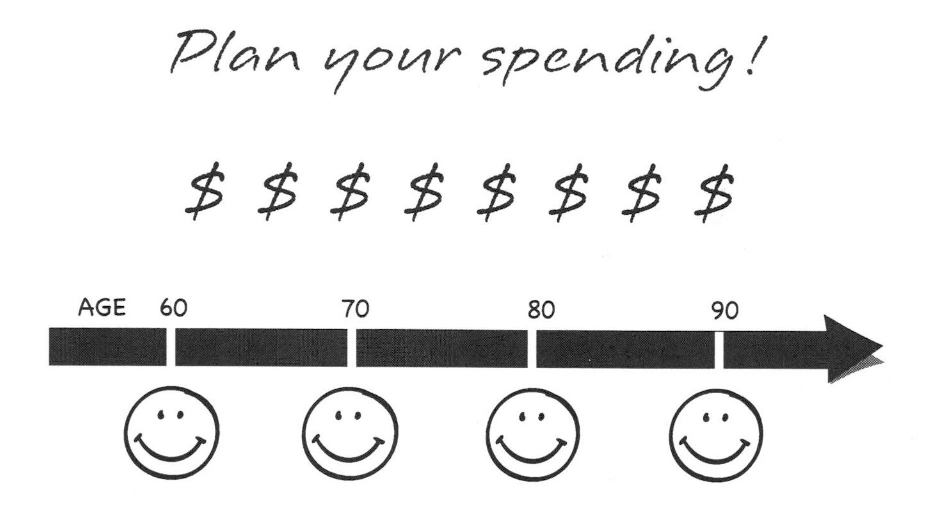

What lessons can we learn from these two stories? My mother and father both made smart choices decades ago that enabled them to enjoy their retirement years without worrying about their money running out. On the other hand, my friend didn't do any planning at all when he retired, an omission he now terribly regrets.

We're headed for a train wreck

If too many boomers follow my friend's example, our nation is headed for a retirement train wreck. It's this type of scenario that keeps me up at night. It also keeps me motivated: I'm dedicated to helping people follow my mother and father's example – to carefully plan for your retirement years in order to be worry-free about having your money last all through your retirement.

For most of your working life, you probably focused your attention on accumulating assets in IRAs, 401(k) plans, and other retirement savings. During your working years, you invested for retirement; you adopted strategies that would help you allocate your assets among stocks, bonds, cash, and other types of investments, while minimizing your ongoing investment expenses.

As you approach retirement, however, you'll want to shift your attention to generating retirement income that will last the rest of your life. But this goal can't be achieved just by using the strategies that worked during your accumulation phase. While asset allocation and minimizing ongoing investment expenses are still important, you'll need to consider other factors as well, such as your expected longevity and the uncertainty of how long you could live, your skill at monitoring your retirement resources, and whether you want to leave a legacy to your children or charities.

You'll also need to make critical decisions about which method or methods you'll use to generate a retirement paycheck from your savings, how you should invest your retirement savings, and which financial professionals and institutions you should select to help you with these critical decisions.

Money for Life can help you make these decisions. In this guide to generating retirement income, you'll learn about the three ways you can generate a retirement paycheck from your savings, the pros and cons of each method, and the many variations on these methods.

Because there's no single solution that works best for everybody, the method that works best for you will depend on your circumstances and goals. And for many people, a combination of methods might work best. So I'll show you how to choose among these methods, given your circumstances and life goals, in order to make the most of your retirement savings.

Generating a secure retirement paycheck is critical for everyone but especially for women

For married couples and committed partners, it's inevitable that one of you will die first, and it's usually the man. Because men tend to marry women a few years younger than themselves and women tend to outlive men by three to five years, if you put two and two together, it's easy to see why most wives can expect a five-to-ten-year period of widowhood at the end of their lives. It's not morbid to plan for this likelihood – it's just prudent.

Accordingly, one very important goal for couples should be the financial security of the survivor; poverty among elderly widows is a real problem in America today. For instance, did you know that a high percentage of widows over age 65 only have income from Social Security? And it's often true that these widows weren't poor until their husbands died.

If you're a single woman, you'll have to be even more vigilant about planning for retirement if you want to be self-sufficient in your retirement years. Having a secure retirement paycheck will go a long way toward achieving this goal.

Women and men tend to think differently about taking investment risks, and adding the risk of outliving your money only complicates the situation. That's why it's critical for women, whether they're single or married, to understand the different methods of generating retirement income when they retire.

Many people want to help, but they can be part of the problem

There are many people who want to help you decide what to do with your retirement savings, and they all have their own biases and points of view. Insurance companies and insurance agents, for instance, typically think annuities (which are an insurance product) are best for generating retirement income, while mutual fund companies, stock brokers, and many financial advisors are more inclined to advise you to invest your savings and make systematic withdrawals to cover your living expenses.

Many financial advisors can also be biased by their training or by the way they bill their clients. As a result, they may only present one or two methods of generating a retirement paycheck. It might be the way that makes them the most money, but that way might not be right for you. Or it might be the method they're most comfortable with based on the limited training they received from their financial institution. The good news is, there are many financial advisors who have integrity and have received specialized training in developing retirement income; your job is to find these advisors and work with them.

Americans appreciate choices, and that's particularly important when it comes to your retirement security. Ideally, your planner will present you with several distinct choices that will allow you to generate a retirement paycheck and will explain the pros and cons of each. So it's crucial that you select a financial planner who has the necessary expertise – and your best interests at heart.

About *Money for Life*

I don't sell annuities, insurance, or investments. What I do is prepare retirement education campaigns, deliver retirement planning workshops, and write about retirement planning strategies, including a thrice-weekly column for CBS MoneyWatch. My recommendations aren't influenced by how I make my money, which enables me to give you an unbiased perspective on the pros and cons of each of the different ways to generate retirement income. I use my training as an actuary[1] and my 35-plus years of experience helping employers design and manage their retirement programs to provide you with the information you need to make smart decisions regarding your retirement income.

To help you more easily understand what your options are, I've organized this book into two parts. Part One covers just the basics on generating retirement income. It summarizes the three primary methods of generating retirement income and provides a framework for making decisions that balance the goals that are relevant to your circumstances. This section gets right to the point and details my five favorite solutions for generating a retirement paycheck.

Part Two is a resource section that goes into more detail on the three primary methods and their varieties, as well as on issues such as taxes, insurance company guarantees, and investing strategies. If you want to learn more about any of the topics covered in Part One or if you'd like to refine your retirement income strategies, you can dig into Part Two to find the information you need there. Or you can choose to skip Part Two and leave these issues to your financial advisor or tax accountant.

Some of you will read this book and other materials on generating a retirement paycheck and will be able to make decisions on your own to craft an income-generating strategy that works for you. If that's the case, more power to you!

Others may feel more comfortable hiring a financial professional to help them with these important decisions. If this sounds like you, then you'll appreciate the information I've included in Part One on choosing a financial professional. This information will not only help you select the most appropriate financial advisor, but it will also provide you with the information you need to have an informed conversation with your advisor, so that together, you can choose the strategies that work best for you.

One thing this book won't do is answer the many other important questions you'll need to ask yourself when planning for your retirement, including:

- when to start drawing your Social Security benefits,
- how to protect yourself from potentially ruinous bills for medical or long-term care expenses,
- how to best deploy your home equity,
- where to live during retirement,
- whether you'll need to work after you retire from your current job,
- what to do with your time, and

- how to remain healthy to help minimize your medical and long-term care expenses and really get the most out of your later years.

There are many other books that offer strategies and ideas for addressing these decisions, including my recent book, *Recession-Proof Your Retirement Years: Simple Retirement Planning Strategies That Work Through Thick or Thin.* You can also learn more about these topics by reading my free, online retirement planning guide, *Money for Life.* These resources present a holistic view of retirement planning on a variety of issues and will help you manage your retirement security. There's also a resource list at the back of this book with many helpful references.

Learning how to generate retirement income from your retirement savings isn't rocket science, but there are enough details that this topic deserves its own book. I sincerely believe that anybody who makes the effort can learn enough to make informed decisions. I've explained things carefully and clearly, and I've used simple descriptions, charts, and illustrations to help you understand this important subject.

It will take many hours of your time, however, to read and really understand the strategies in this book and to do your own research about the products and services that best meet your specific goals. But don't let the amount of time or effort you'll need to put in dissuade you from starting. You're setting up your financial security for the next 20 years or more, and it's going to take some time and patience to do the job right.

Remember, this is one of the most important financial decisions you'll make in your entire life. For this reason, I'd suggest that you include your spouse or partner in this effort, so that he or she has input into your plans and can continue them if they should survive you.

In the long run, the time you spend now will be well worth the effort. If you're ready, let's get started.

---

[1]Actuaries are professionals who measure the risks of important but unpredictable life events – risks such as death, serious illness, accidents, and outliving your money during retirement (living too long is considered a risk!). We design financial programs to mitigate these risks, such as life insurance, medical insurance, pension plans, and 401(k) plans. As part of our training, we study the mathematical chances of these life events happening, along with the types of investments and financial products and services that will protect individuals from the adverse consequences of these events. We've been called the "architects of financial security."

PART ONE

THE BASICS

$ $ $ $ $ $ $ $ $

Your money

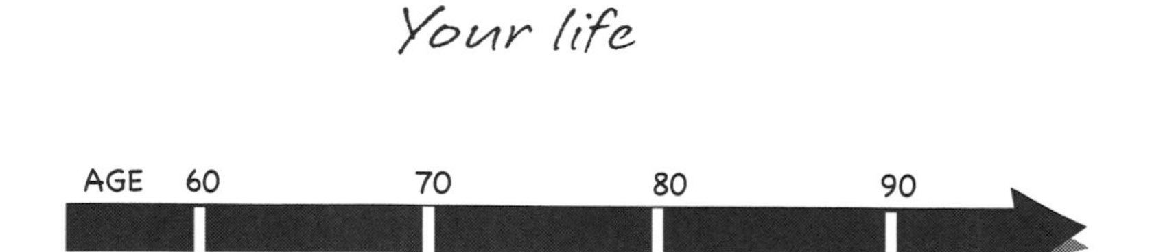

CHAPTER 1

The *Money for* LIFE™ Five-Step System

It's safe to say, most people live paycheck to paycheck while they're working without planning too far ahead financially. They think they'll be fine as long as they've got their monthly expenses covered, because they assume their paycheck is relatively secure and will keep coming in indefinitely.

"Planning ahead" for these people might consist solely of setting aside money for expenses that occur less frequently than monthly, such as property taxes, homeowner's insurance, and so on. If they've thought ahead a little more than that, they might also have saved money for unforeseen emergencies or for longer-term goals, such as a down payment on a house, college tuition for their children, and regular savings from their paycheck for retirement.

Many people have successfully managed to survive their working years using the strategy described above. If you're one of these lucky ones, good for you! But no matter how well you managed your money during your working years, you'll need to change your strategy when you're planning for your retirement. After all, you can no longer count on that regular monthly paycheck coming in. Instead, you'll need to replace the monthly paycheck you got from your employer with a monthly paycheck you generate from the financial resources you've set aside for retirement, a paycheck that will continue coming in for the rest of your life. And while that's a sobering thought, it's a critical goal when planning for your retirement.

Living paycheck to paycheck while you were working imposed a necessary financial discipline on your spending – that's actually good training for retirement, so you shouldn't change that discipline after you retire. Letting go of this financial discipline was a big part of my friend's problem, which I described earlier in the Introduction.

Before we dig into the particulars of how to generate a lifetime retirement paycheck, however, it's important that you do some homework first. Consider that when painters do their job properly, they spend time sanding and prepping before getting out the paint, rollers, and brushes. In the same vein, you'll need to do some prep work to get ready for the crucial task of choosing the best methods of generating retirement income, income that will last as long as you live no matter what happens in the economy.

Determining the retirement income solution that will work best for you is part art, part science. To help you craft a plan that's all your own, let me start by sharing my ***Money for* LIFE™** five-step system that can help you choose the best retirement income solution for you. This process not only helps you determine how much money you'll need to retire and when you can afford to retire, but includes steps you'll need to take to plan your overall retirement, not just generate an ongoing paycheck from your retirement savings.

The steps on this list help you balance what I call "the magic formula for retirement security":

I > E, or

Income > Expenses

The goal is to make this formula work every year for the rest of your life.

Now let's get started with my five-step system.

Step 1: Estimate your life expectancy.

When planning for your retirement, you first need to estimate how long you might live and, if you're married or in a committed relationship, how long your spouse or partner might live. I think this is a natural first step because without having at least an estimate of your lifespan or that of your partner, it's hard to figure out just how long your retirement paycheck will need to last.

You can get an idea of how long you might live by determining your life expectancy. Your expected longevity is influenced by both your lifestyle and your genes; you have to take both factors into account in order to get the most accurate picture of how long you might live.

Either of these two informative websites – www.livingto100.com or www.bluezones.com – can help you estimate your life expectancy. On these sites, you answer questions about your diet and exercise habits, your social life, and your family history; each site then determines a life expectancy that's customized to your circumstances. They'll even make suggestions for improving your results through changes in your lifestyle!

After getting the results of a life expectancy estimator, many people are surprised to learn how long they might actually live, either due to general misunderstandings about life expectancies or because they'd already guessed how long they might live based on the ages that their parents or older relatives died. But guessing isn't the best solution – instead, it's important to get a more realistic idea of just how long your retirement paycheck may need to last and of the range of possible longevity outcomes for your life. Because you want your money to last as long as you do, knowing how long you might live – even if it's just an estimate – can help you make more informed choices about your money.

It's also important to keep in mind that all estimates of your life expectancy are just that – "estimates" based on a number of assumptions. It's entirely possible you could live beyond your life expectancy. It's also entirely possible you'll fall short.

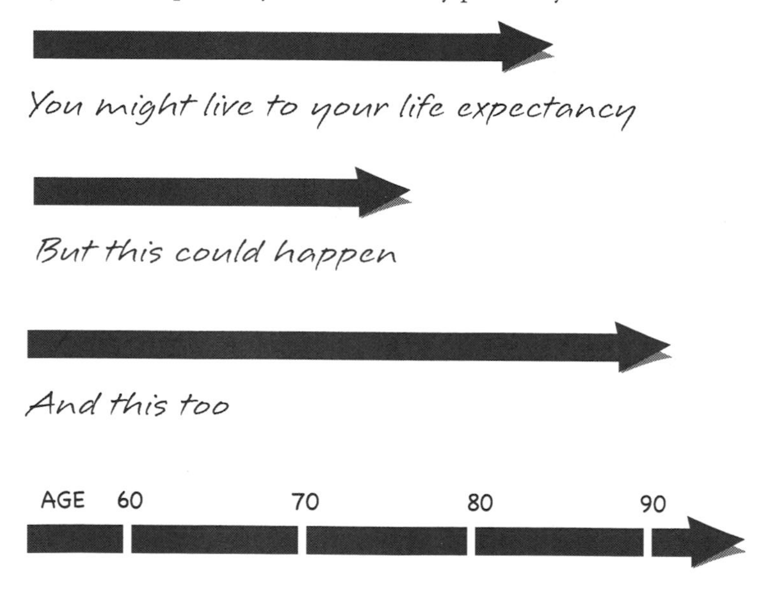

Additionally, it's essential that we clear up some misunderstandings about life expectancies. Some of you may have heard that the average life expectancy in the United States is an age somewhere in the high 70s, leading you to conclude that if you retire at age 65, your money only needs to last 10 to 15 years. But you might have reached the wrong conclusion, and in the wrong direction, when it comes to generating retirement income. That's because these general numbers are the life expectancies *at birth*, and statisticians average in everybody who will die in childhood and in early to mid adulthood.

If you've reached your 60s, you're in a more elite group regarding longevity compared to *all* the people who were born the same year as you, since you've managed to survive for at least 60 years. What you should be interested in is the *remaining* life expectancy for someone your age.

Table 1.1 shows the remaining life expectancies at ages 60, 65, and 70, based on mortality tables from the Society of Actuaries. These life expectancies use mortality rates that are appropriate for people currently in their 50s and 60s. According to Table 1.1, half the population will survive at least as long as the number of years shown (this is known as the median result):

TABLE 1.1 REMAINING YEARS OF LIFE FOR HALF THE POPULATION

Age	Men	Women
60	22 years or more	25 years or more
65	18	21
70	14	16

But remember: These are just averages. What you really need to know are the odds of beating these averages and living beyond the remaining life expectancies shown. For example, there's a 25% chance that a 65-year old man will live another 23 years, and a 5% chance that he'll live another 28 years. Similarly, there's a 25% chance that a 65-year old woman will live another 26 years, and a 5% chance she'll live another 31 years.

But what is it that helps you beat these averages? There are numerous factors to take into account. For instance, you're likely to live longer than average if you have above-average income, you have above-average educational levels, your older relatives lived beyond average life expectancies, you keep your weight at a healthy level, and you don't smoke or abuse alcohol.

If you're interested in learning more about the odds of living to various ages, you can find a simple life expectancy calculator on the website of the Society of Actuaries. Just do an Internet search on the term "simple life expectancy calculator Society of Actuaries."

In addition to understanding how long your retirement paycheck will have to last, having a more accurate picture of your life expectancy can also influence which method or methods you'll use to generate that paycheck. For example, if you expect to live a long time, you might consider purchasing an annuity from an insurance company that promises to pay you a monthly paycheck for the rest of your life. If you don't expect to live a long time, however, buying a lifetime annuity from an insurance company may not be a good deal for you and you may want to choose a different method of generating retirement income.

Knowing how long you might live can also motivate you to plan ahead for the many years you might have left. Too many people just plan a few months or a few years ahead. When you retire, you'll need to lengthen your planning horizon to 20 years or more.

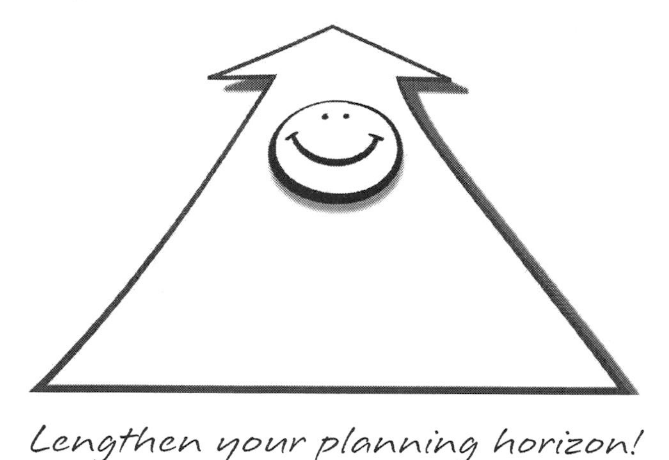

Lengthen your planning horizon!

Step 2: Take inventory of your retirement resources.

Your next homework task is to take inventory of your sources of retirement income. You should start by organizing and determining the current value of all your retirement savings accounts, including IRAs, employer-sponsored plans such as 401(k) plans, and regular savings that aren't held in a tax-advantaged account. Be sure to include your spouse or partner's accounts, if applicable.

Another important part of this inventory is to determine how much lifetime retirement income you can expect to get from sources other than your own savings, such as Social Security or an employer-sponsored pension (if you're lucky enough to participate in such a plan).

You can get estimates of your Social Security income, based on your wage history, at the Social Security website, www.ssa.gov/estimator. The "Retirement Estimator" on this site will show you what Social Security income you can expect to get at various starting ages. If you're married or in a committed relationship, you might want to have your spouse or partner estimate their income, too.

Determining the best age at which to begin drawing your Social Security benefits isn't always easy. Although you'll get more income if you delay starting benefits beyond age 62 (the earliest possible age you can start benefits), there will be a number of factors involved in your decision, including whether you'll continue working in your 60s and 70s, whether you'll draw a pension from work, and how much other money you've managed to save for retirement. But knowing the answers to all these questions can help you decide at just what age you should begin Social Security. It will also help you make the best choice when it comes to selecting a method that will help you generate a lifetime retirement paycheck.

Many financial advisors and writers, including me, advocate that you should delay taking Social Security income for as long as possible (but no later than age 70). This can increase your security in retirement, as well as the security of the surviving spouse, which is often the wife. But if you adopt such a strategy, you may need some other retirement income until the age at which you're planning to start your Social Security benefits. This additional income can come from part-time work or, if you're fully retired, may need to come from your retirement savings. This, too, will influence the strategy you choose for generating your retirement paycheck.

Detailing all the different Social Security claiming strategies is beyond the scope of this book, but you can learn more about them from my companion book, *Recession-Proof Your Retirement Years,* my free online retirement planning website www.moneyforlifeguideonline.com, or other websites, including www.socialsecuritychoices.com or www.socialsecuritytiming.com.

The next part of Step 2 is only for those of you who participate in a defined benefit pension plan at work. This type of plan will provide a significant retirement paycheck that's guaranteed to last for the rest of your life. If you've participated in such a plan, your next task is to get estimates of the amount of money you can expect to receive from this plan after you retire. Many employers have online retirement planning websites that will let you estimate the amount of your pension at various starting ages; you can also get this information by calling your plan administrator.

Knowing how much guaranteed, lifetime income you'll get from both Social Security and your employer-sponsored pension will most likely influence which methods you choose to generate a retirement paycheck from your IRA, 401(k), and other retirement savings. By determining those amounts first, you'll begin to see just how much other money you'll need to cover your expenses.

Step 3: Figure out how much money you'll *really* need.

It's now time to estimate your living expenses during retirement. After you retire, your living expenses can change dramatically from what they are now. For example, they can decrease in retirement if:

- You no longer have children living with you.

- You aren't saving for retirement anymore.
- You don't pay FICA taxes, and your income taxes are reduced.
- You don't have any work-related expenses.
- You're spending less on transportation, possibly by owning just one car or by using public transportation more often.
- You pay off the mortgage on your current house, downsize to a smaller residence, or move to a less expensive part of the country.

On the other hand, your retirement living expenses can increase if:

- You're paying more for health care or health insurance, or you anticipate a need to pay for long-term care.
- You have dependent parents who need long-term care (and your financial help).
- You have children who need your financial help.
- You're traveling more or are participating in additional recreational activities and hobbies.
- You spoil your grandchildren with trips or expensive "toys," or even help out with their college expenses.

In order to determine how much money you'll really need after you retire, it's important to estimate how your living expenses will change in retirement as part of your homework. You should estimate your *essential* living expenses for items such as rent, mortgage payments, utilities, food, and insurance, and then estimate your *discretionary* expenses for items such as vacations, hobbies, and eating out. Be sure to include routine, monthly living expenses as well as expenses paid less frequently, such as property taxes or homeowners insurance, when you're calculating your essential living expenses.

You can get help estimating your retirement living expenses with online software, such as Fidelity's Retirement Income Planner or Quicken. You can also find worksheets to help you in the Resources section of my website, www.restoflife.com.

One important item to be sure to include is your estimated out-of-pocket expenses for medical care, including premiums for Medicare. These expenses will most likely take a much larger portion of your living expenses during retirement than when you were working. To help you calculate those figures, you can use the online system developed by HealthView Services, which estimates your medical expenses in retirement. This calculator can be found at www.hvsfinancial.com.

Knowing the amount of your essential and discretionary living expenses can definitely influence the methods you'll choose to generate a retirement paycheck from your savings, as you'll see later in this book.

And now it's time to take a homework break. The final two steps – choosing the method(s) you'll use to generate a retirement paycheck and estimating your retirement number – will need to be done after you've finished reading Part One. Continue reading below, so you'll know what homework you'll be working on at the end of Part One, but understand that you'll need to read first and work on your homework later.

Step 4: Decide which method or methods you'll use to generate a retirement paycheck.

There are many ways to generate a retirement paycheck, each with its pros and cons. Because each method generates a different amount of retirement income, you'll need to examine each method closely to see if it will produce enough retirement income to cover your living expenses. The next six chapters (Chapters 2 through 7) describe the different ways you can use your retirement savings to generate an ongoing income and detail their pros and cons.

Chapters 8 and 9 each offer a straightforward way to evaluate and choose the retirement income-generating method(s) that will work best for you. Chapter 8 helps you prioritize various goals you may have and suggests methods of generating retirement income that meet each of the goals that is important to you. It also helps you estimate how much retirement income you can expect to get from the various retirement income-generating methods. Chapter 9 outlines a basic "win/regret" analysis, showing situations in which you win and situations in which you might regret your choice of retirement income solutions.

Step 5: Estimate your retirement number.

Once you decide how much of a retirement paycheck you'll need to cover your living expenses and just how you'll generate that retirement paycheck, you can estimate how much retirement savings it will take to generate that paycheck. Chapter 10 will help you finish this five-step list, so you can learn when you can really afford to retire.

One thing to keep in mind: After you complete this process for the first time, you may not be satisfied with the outcome. If that's the case, it might make sense to repeat the process after making adjustments in the various steps as often as you need until you reach an action plan that feels right for you.

What do you *really* need – or want?

It can be a very insightful exercise to see how long you might live and to realistically estimate your living expenses during retirement. In addition to helping you determine how much retirement income you'll need, this information may also influence whether you continue to work part time or retire completely. When you're trying to determine how much money you think you'll need during retirement, you may want to seriously ask yourself how much money you *really* need to be happy. Is it worth your freedom to cut back on your lifestyle during your retirement? Or could you work a little during your retirement years and still be happy?

Remember, if you retire full time in your mid-60s, it's quite possible that your money might need to last for 25 years or more. It could take a boatload of savings to generate a retirement paycheck that will last this long. In addition, a lot can happen in the economy during this time – things that are beyond your control and that can drain your retirement savings.

Depending on the goals you have for retirement, you may decide that it makes sense to continue working until your late 60s or early 70s, so that you're relying solely on your retirement savings for a shorter period, say 15 to 20 years, rather than 25 years or more. If you decide to do this, you won't need as much in savings compared to retiring at an earlier age; the period of time during which you're exposed to economic meltdowns is also shorter.

If working longer in order to afford the retirement you really want makes sense to you but you don't want to continue in your current working situation, you have options. You can look for different work or find ways to reduce the hours you work at your current job. You may need to be creative and resilient, so you can be happy and financially secure in your retirement years.

You'll want to keep all these possibilities in mind as you investigate how to generate a lifetime retirement paycheck. These factors will influence when you retire, how much retirement savings you'll need, and how you'll generate a retirement paycheck from your savings.

Keep on task

One last thought: It's important to maintain your motivation and enthusiasm for this critical project. You'll need to spend many hours studying and analyzing the various methods it takes to generate a retirement income. To help you keep on task, consider adopting some tips from the study of behavioral finance.

One creative way to do that is to see a picture of yourself that's been aged by a few decades. Recent research has shown that people who see their "future self" are more motivated to take care of themselves. You can find online software, like the iPad app AgingBooth, that will age your photo by typing the term "face aging software" into a search engine. After you've used the software, tape a picture of your future self to your computer monitor or your mirror to keep up the enthusiasm and energy you need to continue the necessary retirement planning. I've done this myself, and it was both scary and inspiring.

You can take this task one step further by imagining what you want to be doing in your later years. Knowing what type of retirement you want can motivate you to make sure you have enough money to make that happen. Writing down your goals can also increase your commitment to take action.

Take care of your future self!

Another tip is to form a small study group of friends and family, including your spouse or partner, who are all in the same boat. Commit to meeting regularly and sharing homework tasks. Research has shown that you'll increase your motivation and willingness to make important changes in your life by "being in this together" with people whom you care about.

Now that you've finished your "sanding and prepping," you're ready to learn more about the various methods for generating retirement income from your savings. And you can either get started on some of the five steps now, or you can wait until you've finished this book. If you decide to start now and complete Steps 1 through 3, you'll be prompted to finish Steps 4 and 5 in Chapter 10 – it circles back to the steps on the list so you can finish completing them.

One last note: Although it's OK to continue reading ahead while you start on this list, don't finalize any decisions about your retirement paycheck until you've finished all your homework – and this book – first.

CHAPTER 2

Three Ways to Generate Lifetime Retirement Income

With the average U.S. life expectancy still rising – and if you do your part to take care of your health – it's quite possible you might live into your late 80s or beyond. If you retire in your 60s that means you could end up being retired for 20 or 30 years, and maybe even longer. That should be a good thing – except if you run out of money in your 70s or 80s!

If you're like most boomers, you haven't put enough away in retirement savings to maintain your current lifestyle, so you'll need to squeeze as much income as possible from what you did sock away. And unless you'll be receiving significant benefits from a traditional pension plan, which provides a lifetime monthly income, you should be obsessed with managing your retirement savings so you don't outlive it.

Your options when you run out of money

- *Move in with kids*
- *Go back to work*
- *Marry a rich person*
- *Live in a tent and eat noodles!*

Unfortunately, when it comes to drawing down their retirement savings, studies have found that instead of planning ahead, many people simply "wing it" – they withdraw what they need for living expenses and hope their money will last. Well, hope is not a good strategy!

Instead of hope, let me introduce you to a better strategy and three methods to draw down and invest any type of retirement savings you have, whether that's a straightforward savings account with no special tax features; a 401(k), 403(b), 457, or cash balance plan; or a traditional or Roth IRA.

The overriding strategy

When it comes to your retirement savings, the most important strategy you can adopt is this:

Don't spend the money in your IRAs, 401(k) accounts, and other retirement savings vehicles during your retirement.

Can that be right? Did I actually mean what I just said? Absolutely! Let me explain. My concern is that after you retire, you'll see that you've accumulated quite a tidy sum to spend during your retirement. It will look like a lot of money, so you'll think you can easily afford to buy that boat or take that expensive cruise you've been dreaming about. You might start spending your retirement savings on the things you've been planning for and pull out whatever you think you need to cover your daily living expenses.

But if you're not careful, you'll have exhausted the balance in your retirement accounts before too many years have gone by. You'll have plenty of years of living left, but you'll be broke and faced with some hard choices: return to work, drastically scale back your living expenses, or move in with your kids.

Instead of spending haphazardly, what you should do is consider your retirement savings to be monthly "paycheck" generators. Then spend no more than the amount of your paychecks. Since most of us live paycheck to paycheck while we're working anyway, adhering to this financial discipline when we retire shouldn't be too hard.

For the sake of convenience, I'm going to call these retirement income generators "RIGs" for short. These RIGS are critical to creating a financially secure retirement. It might help to think of your RIG as a vehicle that will go the distance and carry you through a secure retirement. As with cars and trucks, RIGs come in several models with a variety of extras that can be customized to suit your needs.

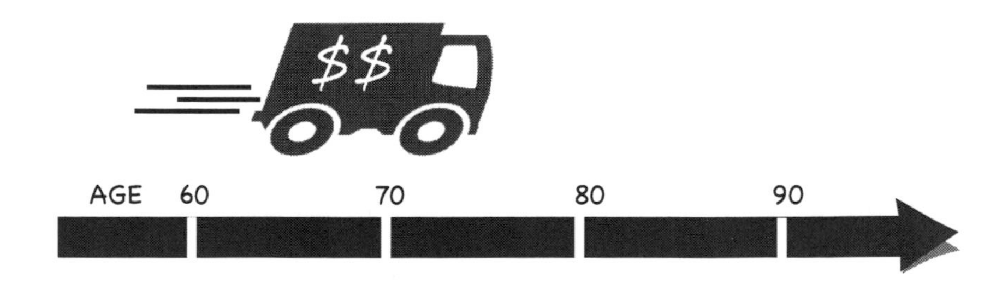

Your RIGs will help you meet your most critical retirement goal:

To develop reliable sources of income that cover your retirement living expenses for the rest of your life, no matter how long you live and no matter what happens in the economy.

If you're married or have a life partner, your retirement paycheck needs to last as long as both of you are alive. Your retirement income also needs to keep up with inflation. While these are ambitious goals, they're what you should be planning for.

In order to achieve these goals, you'll piece your retirement income together from four possible sources:

1. Social Security
2. Pensions
3. Retirement savings
4. Work

For most people, the most important of these – and the one you have the most control over when it comes to generating your monthly retirement paycheck – is your retirement savings. But using your savings to generate a lifetime income can be the most difficult retirement planning challenge for many people, one that requires time and effort – and maybe a little outside help. That's why this book focuses on this single income source and shows you the different ways you can use your retirement savings to generate a monthly paycheck that lasts as long as you live.

Not all of your retirement savings needs to go into a RIG

Before you start using your retirement savings to generate income that will cover your normal living expenses, you should set up an easily accessible reserve for emergencies or for large future expenditures that won't be paid for from your regular retirement paycheck. This amount should be separate from the money you'll use to generate your monthly retirement income.

You'll use this emergency fund for such expenditures as a new car, future home repairs – such as a new roof or water heater – or deductibles and copayments for unforeseen medical costs. You shouldn't need to set aside money for minor emergencies or small unpredictable expenditures, such as minor house or auto repairs, that can be paid from your regular retirement paycheck. Setting aside several thousand dollars should be enough for an emergency reserve, but the amount you ultimately decide on will depend on your specific needs and circumstances.

You might also want to set aside some of your retirement savings if you decide it's a smart strategy to delay your Social Security benefits to maximize your lifetime payout, as I mentioned in Chapter 1. Social Security has some unique features that are hard or expensive to duplicate on your own: It provides a monthly paycheck that's guaranteed to last for the rest of your life, no matter how long you live, and it increases for inflation. In addition, a portion of your Social Security benefits is excluded from your taxable income – at least 15%, maybe more, depending on your total taxable income.

If you decide to delay taking Social Security income, you might need some additional cash to make up for the amount of Social Security income you're delaying. To implement this strategy, decide how much extra income you need for this purpose and set this amount aside. For example, if you could have received $18,000 per year from Social Security at age 62 but you're delaying Social Security benefits for four years, set aside $72,000 and invest it in a short-term interest-bearing account. Another possibility is simply to work just enough to cover these amounts, and then you won't need to set aside this money.

The rest of your retirement savings is fair game for generating a retirement paycheck, so let's now look at the three basic methods you can use to do this.

The three types of RIGs

There are essentially just three ways to generate a monthly paycheck from your retirement savings:

1. Invest your savings, and spend just the investment earnings, which is typically interest and dividends. Don't touch the principal.

2. Invest your savings, and draw down the principal cautiously, so you don't outlive your assets. In this book, I'll call this method "systematic withdrawals."

3. Buy an immediate annuity from an insurance company and live off the monthly benefit the insurance company pays you.

These three methods are all designed to generate a lifetime retirement income, no matter how long you live; achieving this goal will help you relax and enjoy your retirement. These methods might also provide protection against inflation – another important goal for many people.

There are many variations on each of these methods. Here are just a few examples:

- If you decide to invest your money and only spend your investment earnings, you can invest in a variety of mutual funds, bank accounts, individual stocks and bonds, or rental real estate.

- If you decide to use the systematic withdrawal method, you can invest your savings on your own and decide how much to draw down, or you can use a managed payout fund that does the investing and withdrawing for you.

- If you decide to purchase an immediate annuity, you have options. For example, you can buy an annuity that's fixed in dollar amounts, one that's adjusted for inflation, or a variable annuity that's adjusted according to an underlying portfolio of stocks and bonds. You can also buy an annuity that starts at a later age, or you can purchase a hybrid annuity that includes some of the features of systematic withdrawals.

These RIGS each have their advantages and disadvantages; there's not one magic bullet that works best for everybody. And you don't need to use just one type of RIG to generate the income you need. In fact, it might be best to use a combination of a few different types. In addition, there can be good reasons to change your RIGs as you get older. And as we'll see in the chapters to come, some financial institutions have been introducing hybrid products and solutions that combine features of two or more of these basic RIGs.

The underlying investments in your RIGs are also a very important aspect to consider. You'll want to take the following features into account: asset allocation, investment costs, historical investment performance, and the performance you might expect in the future. To help you understand these aspects, I'll cover them all in more detail in Part Two.

Built to last

If your retirement lasts 20 years or more, it's sobering to think that your retirement income will need to withstand likely future meltdowns in the economy. I say "likely" because if we look at the 25-year period from 1987 to 2012, there have been four major meltdowns during this time, each one packing a potential knockout blow to retirees hoping to live on their retirement savings. So it's both smart and possible to set up your RIGs so they'll continue cranking out retirement income during future meltdowns. The different types of RIGs each have their degrees of protection from market meltdowns, which we'll cover in the chapters detailing each of the three RIGs.

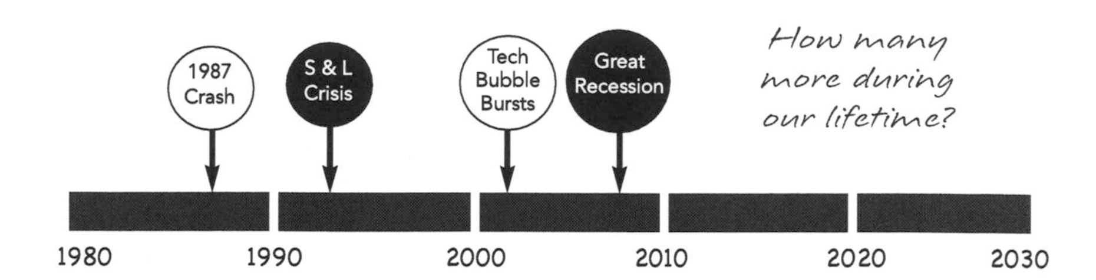

Important tradeoffs between your LIFE goals

Before we begin digging into the three types of RIGs to see exactly how they work, it's essential to understand the important tradeoffs you'll face when choosing your specific RIGs. Some of these tradeoffs focus on the degree of control you want over your retirement savings vs. the certainty that your retirement paycheck will last the rest of your life, no matter how long you live and no matter what happens in the economy.

It's important to realize two cold, hard truths: You'll most likely need to make some tradeoffs between the goals described below. And these tradeoffs will have a significant impact on the amount of retirement income you'll receive.

Some people will opt for a retirement income with lifetime guarantees that isn't subject to the risk of poor investment performance. Others might be willing to live with some uncertainty in exchange for the ability to have some control over and access to their retirement savings, and for the potential to leave a legacy to their children or charities. As we investigate your options, I'll elaborate on these tradeoffs in the chapters that follow.

Let's look a little deeper at the possible goals you'll set when it comes to your RIGs. I call these the **LIFE** goals:

- **Longevity protection:** Is your retirement income guaranteed to last for the rest of your life, no matter how long you live?
- **Inflation protection:** Does your retirement income have the potential to grow so you can keep up with inflation?
- **Flexibility and the potential for a Financial legacy:** Can you withdraw your savings in case of emergencies or for special spending needs, or to be

able to make changes in the way you generate retirement income? When you pass away, are unused funds available for a legacy to your children or charities? While these may appear to be two different goals, with most RIGs, these goals go hand-in-hand and deliver the same outcome. So for simplicity's sake, I've combined them into one goal.

- **Exposure to market risk is minimized:** Is your income protected from stock market crashes or increases in long-term interest rates?

Most people want to maximize the amount of their retirement income and satisfy as many of these goals as possible with their RIGs. Unfortunately, you get what you pay for when it comes to addressing these goals. What I mean is, the more of these goals you want to meet, the lower your initial retirement income will be. The ***Money for* LIFE™** retirement rating system uses these goals as a framework for helping you decide which RIG, or combination of RIGs, will work best for you given your particular circumstances.

Tradeoffs: goals vs. amount of income

There's one more thing to consider: When selecting a specific RIG, you'll need to make a trade-off between the **LIFE** goals and the amount of retirement income you need. For example, a 65-year-old with $500,000 in retirement savings can reasonably expect to generate an annual retirement income of between $15,000 and $30,000, depending on the RIG they use and how many goals they want to address. These net figures correspond to the initial annual retirement incomes equaling 3% and 6% of savings, respectively – this book refers to these percentages as the "payout rates."

The $15,000 amount meets the most number of **LIFE** goals and gives you *maximum control* over your retirement investments. The $30,000 amount addresses the fewest number of **LIFE** goals and gives you the *least control* over your retirement investments, but it also *maximizes the certainty* of your retirement income. As you continue to read this book and work through your homework tasks, you'll have to decide just which goals are most important to you.

Shopping tips

Once you decide on the retirement paycheck solution you think will work best for you, you'll need to work with one or more financial institutions to implement the specific RIG you'll use. Below are three additional goals – important no matter what type of RIG you need – that you may want to consider when going investment shopping.

These goals don't necessarily affect the initial amount of retirement income you receive. Instead, they affect how much of your savings you'll keep during your lifetime, and they help protect against the "leakage" that can drain your retirement savings.

1. **Protect against fraud and mistakes.** How likely is it that you'll make a mistake that causes you to lose part or all of your retirement income? Even worse, is it possible for someone to defraud you, wiping out all your investments? The goal of keeping your savings protected might not be important initially, but it may gain importance as you age and become less able to manage your investments. It may also be important if you want to ensure that your spouse or partner, who may not be as skilled as you are at managing investments, will be able to easily handle the ongoing maintenance should you die first.

2. **Minimize the expense and effort needed for set-up and ongoing maintenance.** You'll want to minimize the amount of expenses you pay to advisors or investment managers, both when setting up your retirement income generator and for ongoing maintenance during the rest of your life. Minimizing your expenses will help your savings last longer.

3. **Protect against institutional bankruptcy.** To keep your savings as safe as possible, you'll want protection against the bankruptcy of the underlying financial institution, whether it's an insurance company, bank, mutual fund company, or other institution.

With each type of RIG, there are steps you can take to manage all of these issues. As a result, they're of secondary importance for deciding *which* RIG or combination of RIGs is best for you. But once you decide which RIG is best for you, you'll want to get the best deal you can and be sure to protect yourself from future problems. In the chapters that follow, we'll cover these goals for each of the three types of RIGs.

Your employer's plan or IRA rollover?

One last thing to consider: If you have retirement savings invested in your employer's plan, such as a 401(k) or 403(b) plan, you'll need to decide whether to use your employer's plan to generate a retirement paycheck or roll your savings into an IRA and generate the paycheck from there. This decision will depend on whether your employer's plan has retirement income options that are appropriate for you or if the investments in your employer's plan are low-cost funds with good investment performance. It may be that you keep some of your retirement savings in your employer's plan and roll over some of your savings to a financial institution that has effective retirement income generators. We'll discuss these considerations for each RIG in the chapters that follow.

The next three chapters describe each of the RIGs in more detail. You'll learn how they work and discover their pros and cons. I'll also bust some common misconceptions that people have about each type of RIG. In Chapter 7, I'll describe my five favorite methods for generating retirement income, some of which combine the use of two RIGs. And in Chapter 8, you'll learn about a process that can help you decide which method, or combination of methods, works best for you.

CHAPTER 3

Retirement Income Generator #1: Investment Income

When it comes to generating a lifetime monthly retirement paycheck, the first type of retirement income generator (RIG) you might consider is one that allows you to invest your savings and use just the investment income, typically interest and dividends, for retirement income. With this method, you don't touch the principal; instead, you only use the investment income to pay for your living expenses.

This method virtually guarantees that you won't outlive your money, since you aren't dipping into your principal. It also offers maximum flexibility and control over managing your retirement resources, with the potential to leave a monetary legacy to your children or to charities when you pass away.

The downside? This method produces the lowest amount of retirement income compared to the other two RIGs described in this book. So you might need a significant amount in retirement savings to make this RIG work for you.

Using the vehicle analogy of RIGs that I introduced in the previous chapter, think of this RIG as a valuable vintage car that you keep going indefinitely with careful maintenance, one that becomes a significant inheritance to pass along to your kids.

How it works

At its most basic, the mechanics of using just interest and dividends to pay for living expenses is pretty simple, particularly if you invest in mutual funds: After selecting an investment vehicle, you simply specify that the income generated from it be deposited electronically into your checking account.

The good thing about this income-generating method is that you don't need to decide which assets to sell to generate additional retirement income, which you must do if you're drawing down principal (the second type of RIG that we'll discuss in the next chapter). The only thing you'll need to be concerned with is the payment frequency of your investments – monthly, quarterly, semi-annually, or annually. Many mutual funds pay their investment income quarterly, although some pay monthly or semi-annually, while others just pay annually. If your fund's frequency is less than monthly, you'll need to spread out the income accordingly to calculate your monthly paycheck.

One thing to note is, if you invest in individual rental real estate, although you'll most likely receive your checks on a monthly basis, ongoing maintenance expenses can cause your net income to vary from month to month, and you'll have to plan accordingly.

A RIG for the third life stage

I really like using this RIG in the "early" years of your retirement – say, in your 60s or early 70s. Retirement planners (including me) consider this period to be the new "third life stage," combining work, renewed learning, and leisure. During this period, you might not need to draw as much from savings because you may be supplementing your dividends and interest payments with part-time work to help make ends meet. Later in life, when you're less able or even unable to work, you can shift to other methods of generating retirement income that produce more money.

This flexibility is a key advantage of this strategy: It enables you to reduce the period of time over which you're withdrawing principal from your retirement savings, which happens with systematic withdrawals as discussed in the next chapter. I'm not comfortable suggesting that anyone draw down their savings principal for periods much longer than 20 years, unless, of course, you start with a very large nest egg. There's just too much that can go wrong economically and politically – not to mention that you might live a lot longer than 20 years. In addition, you may experience unexpected needs for your money, say, if your children or parents need financial help. If there's a strong possibility that you'll live into your 90s – and you'll find this out when you estimate your life expectancy as part of the homework I've assigned you – you may want to delay drawing down principal until your 70s in order to make your money last.

Another serious reason to use this RIG

If you decide not to buy long-term care insurance and don't have any other substantial financial resources to pay for long-term care, such as home equity, you may want to consider using this RIG. By not tapping the principal of your retirement savings, you can use it as a reserve in case you eventually need to pay for expensive long-term care.

Everybody should have a strategy to address the threat of potentially ruinous long-term care expenses, and I suggest you address this possibility at the same time you select your RIGs. The manner in which you address the long-term care threat can influence your choice of RIGs and may also influence your budget for living expenses. Although the topic of long-term care is a critical one, it's beyond the scope of this book. If you'd like more details on how to address long-term care planning, see my book, *Recession-Proof Your Retirement Years*, or my online retirement planning guide, *Money for Life*.

One last reason to use this RIG

Using just investment income to pay for your living expenses is one way to partially recession-proof your retirement income. Various studies have shown that the interest and dividend income from a portfolio balanced between stocks and bonds doesn't drop during a market meltdown nearly as much as the underlying value of the portfolio. So if you can tolerate a modest drop in your income if a market meltdown strikes, you won't be forced to sell at a market bottom – a sure way to lose lots of money. By learning to live with a little less during a market downturn, you'll preserve the bulk of your savings, thus recession-proofing your retirement income.

How does investment income meet the LIFE goals?

Depending on the types of investments you choose, this RIG method meets two or three of the four **LIFE** goals previously described in Chapter 2:

- **Longevity protection:** ***Yes.*** Since you aren't withdrawing principal, you have a very high likelihood of not outliving your retirement savings.
- **Inflation protection:** ***Yes or no, depending on the investment you choose.*** Stock investments have the potential to increase your income with growth in dividends. However, there's also the potential to lose money if dividends are cut due to a downturn in the economy, which is what happened in the 2008-2009 downturn. Real estate investments also have the potential to increase your income, but like stocks, they offer no guarantees. Income from bonds typically won't increase for inflation, except for inflation-indexed securities.
- **Flexibility and potential for a Financial legacy:** ***Yes.*** With this RIG, a key goal is to hold your principal in reserve for unexpected expenditures, such as long-term care expenses or emergencies. You also have the flexibility to

adjust to a different drawdown strategy as you age or if your financial situation changes. Since you aren't drawing down principal, it's also likely you'll be able to leave a legacy to your children or charities, if that's important to you.

- **Exposure to market risk is minimized:** ***Yes or no, depending on the investment you choose.*** To achieve the potential for your investments to grow and for your income to increase, you'll need to take some market risk. If you invest in stocks, an economic downturn can cause the amount of your dividends to decrease; declining interest rates can also reduce the amount of interest you earn. On the other hand, if you invest in bonds, particularly government bonds, and you hold them to maturity, there's a very good chance you'll get the principal and interest that's promised regardless of what happens in financial markets.

Specific RIG examples

If you decide to utilize this first type of RIG and can tolerate the risk of drops in your income stream and the value of your retirement savings due to market downturns, then consider a no-load mutual fund with low operating expenses that invests in dividend-paying stocks with the potential for growth in income to protect against inflation.

While an exhaustive analysis of these types of funds is beyond the scope of this book, here are a few examples of low-cost, dividend-paying funds that have a four- or five-star rating (five being the highest rating) from Morningstar as of July 2012:

- Vanguard's Dividend Growth (VDIGX) or Equity Income (VEIPX) funds
- T. Rowe Price's Dividend Growth (PRDGX) fund

Fidelity, Vanguard, and Schwab all offer low-cost stock index funds that also pay dividends and are rated four stars by Morningstar as of July 2012.

If you want more protection against market volatility with a little higher income, consider a mutual fund balanced between stocks and bonds. Examples of such funds that have been rated four or five stars by Morningstar as of July 2012 include:

- Vanguard's Wellesley Income (VWINX), Wellington (VWELX), Balanced Index (VBIAX), or Target Retirement Income (VTINX) funds
- T. Rowe Price's Retirement 2005 (TRRFX) and other target date funds

- Fidelity's Strategic Dividend and Income (FSDIX), Balanced (FBALX), or Puritan (FPURX) funds

Finally, if you want to diversify your retirement income stream, consider investing a portion of your retirement savings in a mutual fund of real estate investment trusts (REITs) that have low costs and a meaningful dividend payout, such as Vanguard's REIT Index (VGSIX) or T. Rowe Price's Real Estate (TRREX) funds. Both were rated three stars by Morningstar as of July 2012.

Retirement income scorecard

To give you a better idea of just how much money you might be able to generate using this RIG, Figure 3.1 shows you the annual retirement income that this type of RIG provided as of July 1, 2012, for some of the specific mutual funds mentioned previously.

As you can see, the annual amount of your retirement paycheck – a.k.a. the payout rate – for this type of RIG varies from a little over 2% to as much as 3.4% of your retirement savings.

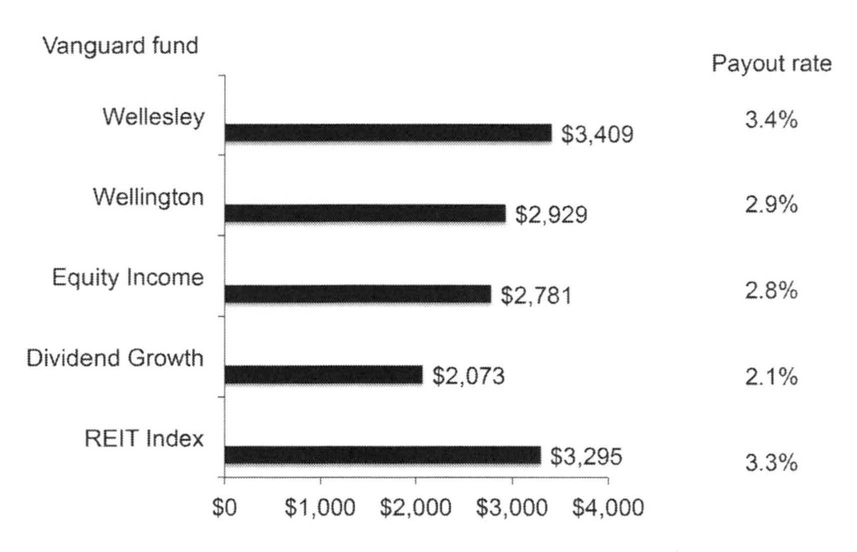

FIGURE 3.1 RETIREMENT INCOME SCORECARD: INTEREST AND DIVIDENDS

Money for LIFE™ goals and amount of retirement income

For the purposes of comparing this method to other RIGs, Figure 3.2 shows you a convenient summary of how investment income meets the **LIFE** goals as well as the initial amount of retirement income that's possible if you invest and spend interest and dividend income only:

Goal	Investment Income
Amount of initial income	○
Longevity protection	●
Inflation protection	◐
Flexibility and Financial legacy	●
Exposure is minimized	◐

● = high or strong
◐ = medium or maybe
○ = low or none

FIGURE 3.2 LIFE GOAL RANKING FOR INVESTMENT INCOME

Shopping tips

To minimize the potential depletion of your retirement savings to fraud, mistakes, and high investment expenses, follow these shopping tips:

- Invest in no-load, low-cost mutual funds that invest in a diversified portfolio that's balanced between stocks, bonds, and cash investments. A no-load fund invests all your money with no commissions subtracted from your investments; with a load fund, you'll pay a one-time commission ranging from 2% to 6% or more to an agent, broker, or financial advisor. This money comes directly from your principal.

- Keep your annual investment expenses well below 50 basis points (0.50%). Often you'll achieve these results by investing in index funds, which invest in stocks or bonds according to a well-known index and don't incur expenses by attempting to outperform the market.

- If you want exposure to real estate for the potential for growth in principal and income, use low-cost mutual funds that invest in REITs.

- Set up automatic deposits so that the interest and dividends are paid electronically to your checking account.

- Periodically, say every year or two, review your investments to make sure they still meet your needs and to keep abreast of new products and services. This may also be a good time to hire a financial planner for a checkup (see Chapter 11 for more thoughts on working with a financial advisor).

- If you invest in bank certificates of deposit (CDs) or standard savings accounts, keep your accounts at each bank below amounts that are guaranteed by the Federal Deposit Insurance Corporation (FDIC); in 2012, these limits are $250,000 per bank, for each type of account ownership category.

You should also investigate the funds that are available from your 401(k) plan at work. Many employers shop for funds that have good investment histories and low expenses. Larger companies can often negotiate deals that aren't available to retail customers, including stable value funds that promise fixed rates of return that are usually higher than the bank CDs available to retail customers.

If you find that your employer has funds with high costs and/or poor investment performance, then you'll want to investigate rolling your accounts to an IRA at a financial institution that offers funds with lower costs and better performance, such as the institutions mentioned earlier in this chapter.

In today's low-interest rate environment, I'd be wary of investing exclusively in bond income funds, particularly if you think you'll switch to another RIG in the near future. If interest rates rise, the market value of your retirement savings could drop right away. This is less of a risk if you're sure you'll stick with this RIG for many years; the reason is that the amount of interest income you'll receive won't change initially, and your interest income could eventually increase over time as the effect of higher interest rates flows into your account.

I'd also shop carefully if you decide to purchase CDs or keep your money in a standard bank savings account. The interest rates are currently too low at most banks to generate much income from these savings tools. If you're serious about CDs or savings accounts, however, you might want to try shopping online to find the highest, FDIC-insured interest rates.

A common misconception

During the many years I've been working as a retirement communicator, I've often heard a common misconception about this method of generating retirement income:

Using just investment income for your retirement paycheck is safe.

Well, not exactly. It's safe in the sense that you're not tapping your principal, but if you invest in risky assets that decline substantially during a market downturn, your investments won't necessarily be safe. The same is true when it comes to investing in CDs at a bank: When CD rates dropped to nearly zero in 2010 and 2011, retirees who relied exclusively on bank CDs for their income got hammered and were forced to dip into their principal.

You might also be tempted to invest for the highest yield you can find. Be aware that high-yield investments often carry risks or hidden fees that can erode your income or the value of your investments. Both Allan Roth and Larry Swedroe, investment experts and fellow columnists for CBS MoneyWatch, offered almost identical advice when I interviewed them for their thoughts on this topic:

"Don't chase the highest yield with junk bonds or other fixed income investments, or the stocks with the highest dividend payouts. You're taking on too much risk, and there's a good chance your payout will drop if the economy turns south."

RIG #1, investment income, works best when you invest in a low-cost, mutual fund that's balanced between stocks and bonds. You'll be subject to some investment risk, meaning there's the possibility that the value of your investments could drop during a market downturn. But it's more likely that your investment income will remain steady or grow over time. And there's a very good chance that your investments will recover from a market downturn, if you've arranged your financial budget so that you can ride out downturns without selling your investments.

If you'd like more details regarding the other issues with this type of RIG, read Part Two of this book. You'll learn more about investment and tax considerations as well as the IRS required minimum distribution (RMD) that's required with traditional IRA and 401(k) accounts.

CHAPTER 4

Retirement Income Generator #2: Systematic Withdrawals

"Spend your last dollar as you spend your last breath."

"Bounce the last check."

"Die broke!"

These are all goals I frequently hear mentioned at my retirement planning workshops from people who are planning to draw down their accumulated IRA, 401(k), and retirement savings accounts to generate retirement income. The first two goals are easier said than done, of course, since nobody knows exactly when they'll die. And while many people will achieve the third goal – dying broke – it won't be because of their stellar planning skills. Instead, they'll be broke for many years before they die because they depleted their retirement savings too rapidly in retirement.

If you need more money than retirement income generator (RIG) #1 – interest and dividends – then consider the second type of RIG I'm suggesting: systematic withdrawals, also known as installment payouts or managed payouts. With RIG #2, you invest your retirement savings in a portfolio that's balanced between stocks and bonds, and then you cautiously draw down both your principal and your investment income to avoid outliving your savings. As you'll see, of the three RIGs available for you to choose from, this one involves the most complex issues, so this will be one of the longest chapters in this book.

Using the vehicle analogy for RIGs introduced earlier in this book, consider this type of RIG similar to a high performance automobile that needs constant maintenance from a *trusted* mechanic to get the best performance regarding speed and gas mileage, and to extend the life of your car. As you've probably experienced, finding a trusted mechanic can be a difficult task – finding a trained, competent financial advisor who has your best interests at heart may be just as challenging.

A few of you might do your own car repairs, but only if you've learned a lot about car mechanics. It's the same with using this RIG – some of you may feel confident enough to implement systematic withdrawals on your own after studying this book and other resources, but many may feel more comfortable working with a trusted financial advisor.

The "safe" withdrawal rate

"Actuarial ruin" is the term used by actuaries to refer to the unfortunate outcome of outliving your money. It's important to realize that once you start drawing down your principal, you run the risk of actuarial ruin – and the more principal you withdraw, or the longer you live, the greater the possibility that you'll experience "money death" before you actually pass away.

Avoid an "out of money" experience!

The "safe" withdrawal rate – so-called because there's an acceptably low risk of actuarial ruin attached to it – is the subject of much debate and analysis. Since you've got to start somewhere, let's consider the well-known "four percent rule" the starting point for your investigation. With the four percent rule, during your first year of retirement, your *annual* retirement paycheck should equal 4% of your retirement savings at the time you retire. You'd then use this annual paycheck as needed over the course of a year to cover your living expenses.

Each year thereafter, you would increase your annual withdrawals to keep pace with inflation, as measured by the increase in the Consumer Price Index (CPI). According to a strict application of the four percent rule, you'd continue giving yourself raises for inflation for the rest of your retirement.

The four percent rule got its start with a landmark paper published in the *Journal of Financial Planning* in 1994 by William Bengen titled "Determining Withdrawal Rates Using Historical Data." Bengen, an author and certified financial planner, used a historical approach to study the effectiveness of this strategy, examining how various withdrawal and asset allocation strategies would have worked in the past given actual history regarding investment and inflation. Here are some key details regarding his approach:

- Bengen looked at annual drawdown percentages that ranged from 1% to 8% of an investor's initial savings.

- He analyzed five different portfolios, ranging from an asset allocation of 100% government bonds to 100% stocks.

- Beginning with the year 1926, he examined all retirement periods that started on January 1 of each year. In other words, he detailed what would have happened if you had retired on January 1, 1926, on January 1, 1927, and so on.

- He then calculated how long someone's retirement savings would have lasted under all these scenarios.

Here are some of Bengen's important conclusions:

- A 3½% withdrawal rate did not produce actuarial ruin for at least 50 years under all scenarios and all retirement periods, resulting in the absolutely safest withdrawal rate.

- A 4% withdrawal rate, coupled with a portfolio that consisted of 50% stocks and 50% bonds, exhausted the retirement savings in 33 years in the worst case, but in most cases, it lasted 50 years or more. Thus Bengen reasoned that a "four percent rule" would offer people the best balance between risk and reward: It was the highest withdrawal rate that could survive the worst scenarios in history for periods of retirement lasting 30 years.

- The 50/50 asset allocation produced the least likelihood of actuarial ruin. But a portfolio with 75% stocks had only slightly higher risks of actuarial ruin, and the significant investment in stocks usually produced higher wealth accumulations than the 50/50 portfolio. This wealth accumulation could be used for legacies to children and charities, something investors often desire. Allocations to stocks of less than 50% and greater than 75% were counterproductive, according to Bengen.

The worst scenarios developed when significant events – such as a large stock market downturn or high inflation – happened early in retirement. These events depressed portfolios so much that it was difficult for them to recover. This worst-case scenario affected retirements that began in the 1960s and 1970s.

The four percent rule has been the subject of extensive analysis and revisions since Bengen published his paper in 1994, including further refinements published by Bengen himself. This investing guideline has attained "rule of thumb" status among many financial planners who use the rationale that the four percent rule has a very low chance of actuarial ruin for retirements that last at least 30 years.

Problems with the four percent rule

Of course, most "rules" aren't problem-free, including this one. Here are a few problems that arise when the four percent rule is strictly applied:

- It doesn't make sense to adopt an investment and withdrawal strategy at the beginning of your retirement, and stick with it rigidly throughout your retirement without considering how your investments have performed during the time you're drawing down your savings. When you're working for a salary, you experience ups and downs in your paycheck over the years and adjust your life accordingly. It only makes sense to do the same with your retirement paycheck, taking into account how well your investments perform and changes in your life circumstances.

- Due to the low interest rate environment in 2012, the four percent rule has been challenged as too high of a withdrawal rate to be considered safe. In addition, a point of view that's emerging among financial analysts is that Bengen's analyses were based on a period of U.S. history that had been remarkable with respect to economic growth and stability; future periods may not produce the same level of growth and stability that could support a 4% withdrawal rate.

- You might need a retirement income that lasts for a period longer than 30 years. For instance, consider that for a married couple in which the husband is 65 and the wife is 62, there's about a one-in-four chance that one of them will live for more than 30 years.

- The analyses that support the four percent rule assume you'll earn the rates of return on common stock and bond indexes without any investment or advisor expenses. In reality, many mutual funds underperform these indices over the long run for two reasons: (1) Investment expenses reduce the net returns to investors, and (2) it's very hard for investment advisors to consistently beat the market averages over long periods of time. And if you're paying a financial advisor from your retirement savings, that creates an additional drag on your investment returns.

As a result of these issues, you'll most likely want to consider variations and adjustments to the four percent rule. Don't just automatically adopt a four percent withdrawal strategy without investigating the potential pitfalls or without considering your life goals and circumstances. And don't just withdraw money willy nilly from your retirement savings without determining a safe withdrawal strategy for your circumstances; surveys show that many retirees are withdrawing at annual rates of 6%, 7%, 8%, or higher, with the likely result that they'll experience "money death" before passing away.

There's one more issue with the four percent rule: It may not produce enough retirement income to cover your living expenses. In this case, you may want to consider using RIG #3, immediate annuities, which you'll learn more about in Chapter 5.

Consequences of using a "safe" withdrawal rate

It's also important to understand the likely consequences of adopting a "safe" withdrawal rate: If you're successful at managing your investments and withdrawals so that you don't run out of money before you die, you'll almost certainly end up with money left over at the time of your death. If your investments have done well or if you die prematurely, you could leave lots of money on the table. On the other hand, if your investments perform poorly, if you live too long, or if you withdraw too much, you could leave a very small legacy, or worse, outlive your money altogether.

But some people would rather have a higher retirement income and not leave too much money behind when they die. Unfortunately, there's no *guaranteed* way to assure that will happen with systematic withdrawals. If this is important to you, you might want to consider an immediate annuity, which has the potential to maximize your retirement paycheck while guaranteeing that you won't outlive your savings. Or you could use a combination of systematic withdrawals and an immediate annuity, which is actually one of my favorite retirement income solutions. We'll delve into the details of immediate annuities in Chapter 5 and my favorite retirement paycheck solutions in Chapter 7.

Digging deeper into the "safe" withdrawal rate

Now it's time to further investigate the odds of failure with the four percent rule. It's often cited that the four percent rule produces a 10% chance – one in ten – of actuarial ruin for a 30-year retirement. Yet consider a couple where the husband is 65 and the wife is 62. The odds are about 25% – one in four – that one of them will still be alive 30 years down the road. Multiply these two odds together, and there's only about a 2½% chance – a little less than 3 out of 100 – that one member of the couple will be alive after 30 years *and* will exhaust their savings. In other words, the odds are pretty low that they'll experience actuarial ruin. And if ruin does happen, it will most likely be in the last few years of their retirement.

Choosing to face that risk is up to you. Some people might be willing to accept a small chance of actuarial ruin near the end of their lives in order to enjoy a higher retirement income. Others might consider any chance of ruin to be irresponsible, particularly if it's likely that it's their spouse or partner who'll still be alive when the money runs out. Put another way, someone who's cautious may feel more comfortable with a 3% or 3½% withdrawal rate, while an optimist may feel perfectly comfortable with a 4% or 5% withdrawal rate.

If you're looking for a higher retirement income, here's the basic tradeoff: You can increase your retirement paycheck with systematic withdrawals by using a withdrawal rate that's higher than 4%, but you'll have to accept a higher risk of actuarial ruin. You can see how this would work in an analysis published in the January 2012 *Journal of Financial Planning* by Wade Pfau, PhD, associate professor at the National Graduate Institute for Policy Studies in Tokyo and director of curriculum for the Retirement Income Industry Association (RIIA). The title of the article was "Capital Market Expectations, Asset Allocation, and Safe Withdrawal Rates." Dr. Pfau analyzed the rates of failure for various withdrawal rates and asset allocations for retirements lasting 30 years. The withdrawal rates shown in Table 4.1 were extracted from his analyses and are applicable to a portfolio invested 50% in stocks.

Table 4.1 Odds of actuarial ruin for various withdrawal rates*

Odds of ruin	Withdrawal rate
5% (1 out of 20)	3.9%
10% (1 out of 10)	4.3%
20% (1 out of 5)	4.9%

**30-year retirement*

According to this analysis, if you withdrew money from savings at a rate of 3.9% (almost 4%), your odds of ruin are only one in 20. But if you increase the withdrawal rate to 4.3%, your odds of ruin double to one in 10. And if you raise that withdrawal rate to 4.9% (almost 5%), your odds of ruin quadruple to one in five.

If you're an optimist, you might think these odds are still pretty low and you'd be willing to take the risk. In this case, you'd need to have a backup plan in place to reduce your withdrawals during your retirement in the event you experience poor returns or live a long time. On the other hand, if you're more the cautious type, the one-in-five odds might seem way too high, particularly if you can't afford to reduce your withdrawals later in retirement.

By the way, Dr. Pfau is quick to point out that the withdrawal rates shown in the above table are based on historical averages that contain a period of U.S. history with remarkable economic growth and stability, and that interest rates on bonds were a lot higher throughout that period than interest rates prevalent in 2012. He cautions against relying on withdrawal rates as high as shown in the table.

While these type of analyses can offer useful information, I wouldn't suggest that anyone rely *too much* on these type of analyses. Before the 2008 - 2009 meltdown, many people easily accepted what they thought was a low chance of actuarial ruin. But the 2008 - 2009 meltdown was one of those "one out of 100" events that actually happened and significantly increased everybody's odds of actuarial ruin. This demonstrates that even with systematic withdrawals, there's no absolute guarantee of protection against severe market downturns.

One thing these analyses *can* do is help you understand how systematic withdrawals work by demonstrating how your odds of ruin increase for different withdrawal rates and retirement periods. They can also be useful in helping you determine an initial withdrawal rate, provided you have a backup plan in place in case there's a significant market downturn.

Finally, keep in mind that the odds of ruin shown previously are the results from just one analyst and his data (albeit a very well-qualified analyst). There are other analysts and financial advisors who use different methods and assumptions of estimating a safe withdrawal rate that produce different results, although the basic concepts are the same and the results are not a lot different. Chapter 14 covers other results as well as online software that will help you refine your withdrawal strategy, if you're seriously considering systematic withdrawals to generate your retirement paycheck.

You gotta have a backup plan!

Several experienced financial analysts have highlighted one circumstance in which you might run out of money with systematic withdrawals: that is, if you experience a substantial downturn in your assets early in your retirement, but rigidly stick to your withdrawal strategy nonetheless by continuing to withdraw the same amounts, increased for inflation each year. In this situation, the odds of actuarial ruin increase substantially. To counter this risk, you must be prepared to reduce your withdrawals if there's a significant drop in your retirement savings.

Larry Swedroe, a financial advisor, author, and blogger at CBS MoneyWatch, has this advice to offer to address the risk of actuarial ruin, particularly if you're using a withdrawal rate higher than 4%:

"You need a backup plan to reduce your withdrawals during a market downturn. Be prepared to pare back your living expenses, go back to work, tap other assets, or move in with your kids."

Here are two ways you can reduce your withdrawals during a market downturn:

1. Reset the dollar amount of your annual withdrawals, based on the reduced value of your savings and the withdrawal percentage that's appropriate for you at that time. This way, if the value of your savings drops, your annual withdrawal drops as well.

2. Don't withdraw any principal during a significant downturn, and limit your retirement paycheck to investment income (RIG #1) only. This way, you won't be forced to sell your assets at a low value at the bottom of the market.

I recommend that you think long and hard about the withdrawal rate that's most appropriate for your age and circumstances, taking into account whether or not you're married or are in a committed relationship. This last consideration impacts how long the retirement paycheck needs to last and whether your survivor is able to continue using your withdrawal strategies. I'd also suggest that any backup plan you create addresses the idea of adjusting your withdrawals to reflect your investment experience as it unfolds during your retirement. This can work to your benefit because you might be able to *increase* your withdrawals in the future if you've achieved very good investment experience over several years.

In order to determine the best withdrawal rate based on your needs and circumstances, it's possible that you'll need to work with a financial advisor who has specific training and experience with analyzing and selecting an appropriate withdrawal rate using systematic withdrawals. A financial advisor can also help you revisit your withdrawal strategy during and following a market downturn or should your needs or circumstances change.

You should now understand one big downside of systematic withdrawals: It requires the most attention from you, compared to the other two RIGs. You'll need to decide which assets to sell to generate your retirement paycheck, and you'll need to periodically revisit your withdrawal rate as you age, taking into account the investment performance of your retirement savings. On the other hand, this RIG also offers two big pluses: You have access to your retirement savings, and it produces a higher retirement paycheck than RIG #1. If the pros outweigh the cons for you, you might want to consider using systematic withdrawals to generate your retirement paycheck.

How systematic withdrawals work

There are two ways you can implement a systematic withdrawal plan:

1. Do it yourself by investing your retirement savings and determining how much you should withdraw so you don't draw down your principal too fast. You may need the help of a financial advisor.

2. Invest in the managed payout fund of a mutual fund company that will do the work – the investing and withdrawing – for you.

Vanguard, Fidelity Investments, Schwab, and other financial institutions all offer managed payout funds, also called monthly income funds or income replacement funds. While these funds certainly offer convenience, proceed carefully if you decide to go this route. The company's decisions on how to invest and how much to withdraw might not be best for you. These funds also have various chances of incurring actuarial ruin, and in some cases, such as Fidelity's Income Replacement funds, the funds are intended to be exhausted by a specified date. Don't blindly invest in one of these funds or rely on the advice of a friend or a neighbor as to which fund to use. Only invest in one of these funds after determining that the fund's withdrawal rate and asset allocation fit your particular circumstances.

If you're not satisfied with the managed payout funds these companies have to offer, then you'll want to investigate how you can do it yourself. Many large mutual fund companies and other financial institutions allow you to set up periodic, automatic, electronic transfers from your IRAs and retirement savings into your checking account. All you'll need to do is specify the:

- amount of each withdrawal,
- frequency of the withdrawals (monthly, quarterly, etc.), and
- specific investments or funds that the withdrawals will come from.

You should also check to see if your 401(k) plan offers this type of automatic payment service. If it does and you like your plan's investment funds, there's no need to roll your 401(k) accounts into an IRA when you retire. Many 401(k) plans, however, don't provide these services, and if that's the case with yours, you'll need to roll your money into an IRA with an institution that allows for periodic payouts.

Which investments should you consider?

To keep it very simple, you could invest all your retirement savings in a target date or balanced mutual fund, both of which invest in a mix of stocks, bonds, and cash. During your research, you'll want to make sure the fund you choose has an average or above-average investment history and very low investment fees. The balanced and target date funds I listed in Chapter 3 meet this criteria. Before searching for funds outside your 401(k) plan at work, however, you should investigate the investments already available in your plan, for the reasons mentioned in Chapter 3.

When you're deciding exactly which investments to choose, it's important to keep in mind that the analyses that support the four percent rule assume you'll earn rates of return equal to historical returns on stock and bond indices without any investment expenses. If you use mutual funds with investment fees that are well above 50 basis points (0.50%) or if your investment advisor charges you fees that equal or exceed this amount, however, you'll need to reduce your withdrawals accordingly, as these fees add up significantly over the years.

Dr. Pfau has a rule of thumb for adjusting your withdrawal rate to reflect expenses for investment management and financial advisors as well as to take into account any anticipated underperformance relative to the indices. He suggests that you reduce your withdrawal percentage by 0.5% for every 1% of underperformance that's reasonable to expect, whether this underperformance is from expenses or because your investments fall below the indices. For example, if you're paying 1% each year to a financial advisor – and that includes investment management fees – then reduce a 4% annual withdrawal rate to 3½%.

It's also a good idea to maintain liquid assets (money market funds and/or bank savings accounts) equal to two to three years' worth of your principal withdrawals. This should help you ride out a market downturn and prevent you from panicking and selling your investments at the bottom of the market just to meet your cash flow needs. We'll talk more about refining your withdrawal strategies and the appropriate investments in Chapter 14 of Part Two.

"You have to be very disciplined with your investing – drive your investment expenses as low as possible with index funds, and remember to rebalance your portfolio periodically."

– **Allan Roth**, financial planning firm founder and blogger for CBS MoneyWatch

One alternative to straightforward systematic withdrawals

Some financial planners use a variation on systematic withdrawals called "age banding" or the "bucket" approach. This approach involves using mostly conservative, fixed income investments for the first 10 years of your retirement, a higher allocation to stocks for the second 10 years of your retirement, and an even higher allocation to stocks for the last 10 years (or so) of your retirement. This investing strategy is designed to help prevent you from panicking during a downturn and selling stock investments at the bottom of the downturn to generate your retirement paycheck.

If you're interested in this approach, consider a refined strategy developed by Dr. Somnath Basu, director of the California Institute for Finance at California

Lutheran University. He combines the above investment strategy with the assumption that your spending will level off or decline as you age. He's developed AgeBander software that projects reduced travel and recreational expenses but higher medical expenses as you get older. You can learn more about his system at www.agebander.com, as well as see a list of financial planners who've been trained on Dr. Basu's AgeBander method.

If you're seriously considering an age banding or bucket strategy, you'll most likely want to work with a qualified financial planner to make this method work. A trained advisor can help you periodically adjust your investments as you age through the "bands" or "buckets" and refine your withdrawal amounts to reflect your changed circumstances. I'd also make sure your advisor takes into account the higher medical expenses you'll experience later in life, possibly by using the AgeBander system developed by Dr. Basu.

How do systematic withdrawals meet the LIFE goals?

Systematic withdrawals meet two of the four **LIFE** goals described in Chapter 2:

- **Longevity protection:** ***No.*** Since you're tapping into principal, there's a chance you could outlive your savings, particularly if you live well beyond your life expectancy and/or experience poor investment returns.

- **Inflation protection:** ***Yes.*** The strict application of this method allows for an increase for inflation each year. However, you may want to cut back on your withdrawals if you experience a downturn in your investments.

- **Flexibility and potential for a Financial legacy:** ***Yes – somewhat.*** You can access your savings for unexpected expenditures, such as long-term care expenses or emergencies. But if you spend this money, it won't be there to generate a retirement paycheck. You also have the flexibility to adjust to a different drawdown strategy as you age or if your financial situation changes. And when you pass away, any unused funds can be a legacy to your children or charities. Just realize that the legacy amount will depend on your investment returns, how much you've withdrawn, and how long you live. The legacy will most certainly be less than with RIG #1 (investment income).

- **Exposure to market risk is minimized:** ***No.*** To achieve the potential for your investments to grow and for your income to increase, you'll need to invest in stocks and take some market risk. If you're invested in stocks, a market downturn can cause the value of your savings to decrease while declining interest rates can reduce the amount of interest you earn.

Retirement income scorecard

Figure 4.1 shows the amount of annual retirement income this type of RIG can generate with $100,000 in retirement savings. The chart details a few sample payout rates for the purposes of comparing the results to other RIGs.

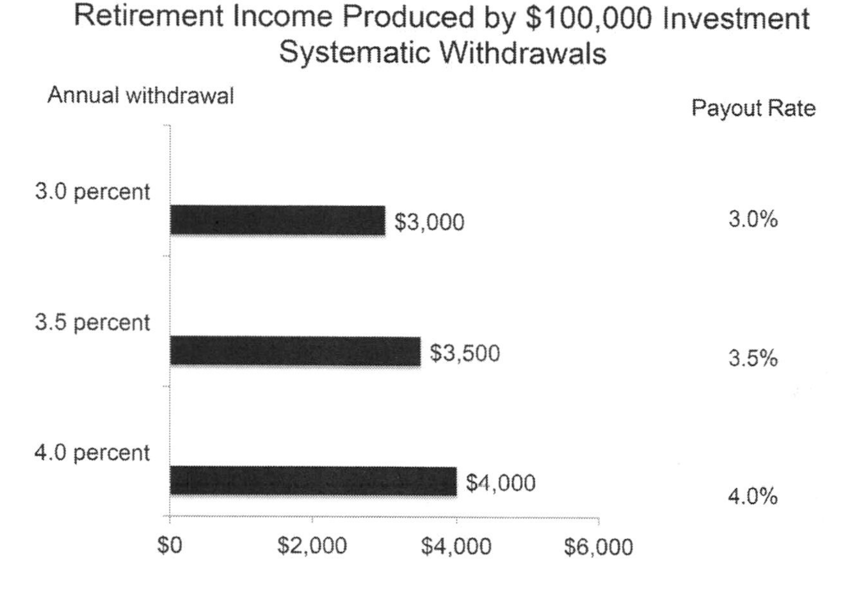

FIGURE 4.1 RETIREMENT INCOME SCORECARD: SYSTEMATIC WITHDRAWALS

Managed payout funds

As mentioned previously, you can implement systematic withdrawals by investing in a managed payout fund of a mutual fund company. Now let's look at the managed payout funds offered by Vanguard and Fidelity. Both of these funds invest your savings in a mix of their other low-cost mutual funds, with asset allocations balanced between stocks and bonds. They do the investing and withdrawing for you, and each month, they'll send you a check that's a combination of investment income and a return of your principal. As you'll see below, Vanguard and Fidelity take very different approaches to their managed payout funds.

Vanguard offers three managed payout funds:

- The Growth Focus fund is invested about 85% in stocks, with the remainder in bonds and cash investments. It had an annual retirement paycheck equal to 2.7% of your savings as of July 2012.

- The Growth and Distribution fund is invested about 75% in stocks, with the remainder in bonds and cash investments. It had an annual retirement paycheck equal to 4.7% of your savings as of July 2012.
- The Distribution Focus fund is invested about 70% in stocks, with the remainder in bonds and cash investments. It had an annual retirement paycheck equal to 6.9% of your savings as of July 2012.

These Vanguard funds have fees that range from 0.34% to 0.46% of assets. They're intended to continue generating monthly payments indefinitely, but that's not guaranteed. The Distribution Focus fund has a withdrawal rate much higher than 4%, so I'd be worried about the risk of ruin with that fund.

Fidelity offers a series of income replacement funds that provide monthly payments of investment earnings and principal. These funds are intended to be exhausted by each fund's target date (hence the snarky nickname they've been given: "target death funds"). The first income replacement fund the company created is intended to go to zero in 2016; succeeding funds have target dates of 2018, 2020, and so on, increasing by two years until the last fund the company currently offers, which has a target exhaustion date of 2042. These funds' annual fees range from 0.54% to 0.67%.

Here's a summary of the payout rate and asset allocation for two of these income replacement funds:

- The 2032 fund is invested about 54% in stocks, with the remainder in bonds and cash investments. It had an annual retirement paycheck equal to about 5.9% of your savings as of July 2012.
- The 2042 fund is invested about 63% in stocks, with the remainder in bonds and cash investments. It had an annual retirement paycheck equal to about 4.6% of your savings as of July 2012.

The payout rates on these funds change every year, depending on the fund's investment performance during the preceding year and to stay on track for exhaustion by the target date.

So why would you select a fund that's intentionally exhausted by a certain date? There are several good reasons:

- You may decide to delay taking your Social Security benefits as a smart strategy to manage the risk of living too long, and you might need some extra income until your Social Security benefits start.

- You might decide to buy longevity insurance – a lifetime annuity that starts at an advanced age, such as age 80 or 85. You could use one of these funds to provide income until that advanced age. This is a hybrid strategy I'll discuss more in Chapters 6 and 7.
- You might choose a target date far in the future – say 2042 – and hope you don't live past that date or plan for other sources of a retirement paycheck.

The Fidelity income replacement funds can be an effective tool for designing an overall strategy for a retirement paycheck, but you obviously need to carefully plan for other sources of income once these funds are exhausted.

Figure 4.2 shows the retirement income scorecard for some of the Vanguard and Fidelity managed payout funds as of July 2012:

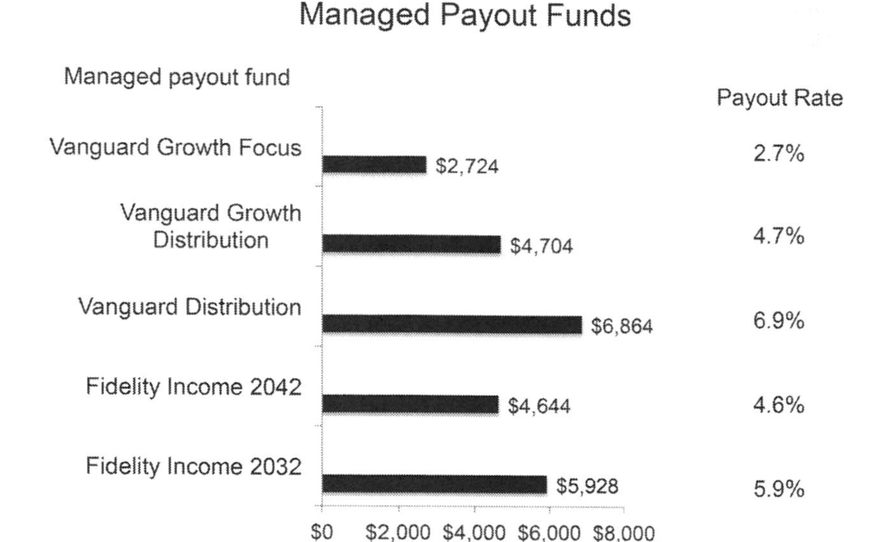

FIGURE 4.2 RETIREMENT INCOME SCORECARD: MANAGED PAYOUT FUNDS

Money for LIFE™ goals and amount of retirement income

For the purposes of comparing this RIG to the other RIGs, Figure 4.2 provides a convenient summary of how systematic withdrawals meet the **LIFE** goals and the initial amount of retirement income that's possible. I've provided rankings for two methods of implementing systematic withdrawals:

1. A cautious withdrawal strategy that starts with an initial low paycheck and then adjusts periodically to reflect investment performance as it develops over your retirement, and

2. An optimistic withdrawal strategy that starts with a higher initial paycheck and makes less frequent adjustments compared to the cautious withdrawal strategy.

Chapter 7 goes into more detail about the differences between cautious and optimistic withdrawal strategies.

Goal	Systematic Withdrawals Cautious	Systematic Withdrawals Optimistic
Amount of initial income	○	◐
Longevity protection	◐	○
Inflation protection	●	◐
Flexibility and Financial legacy	●	◐
Exposure is minimized	◐	○

● = high or strong
◐ = medium or maybe
○ = low or none

FIGURE 4.3 LIFE GOAL RANKING FOR SYSTEMATIC WITHDRAWALS

Shopping tips

RIG #2 has similar investment shopping considerations as RIG #1, so you may want to review the relevant section in Chapter 3 for tips. Here are some additional considerations:

- Don't automatically choose the managed payout fund with the highest payout rate. The payout rates are the same for all customers, regardless of their age, tolerance for risk, or other circumstances. Decide on a withdrawal rate and asset allocation that you're comfortable with, and if you find a managed payout fund that fits your goals, then go for it. Otherwise, you could be better served doing these calculations yourself, possibly with the help of a qualified financial advisor.

- Similarly, don't choose financial advisors who promise the highest withdrawal rate. These advisors won't deliver a high rate because of their investing or planning genius – you'll get it because they've talked you into accepting a higher risk of ruin. Instead, look for advisors who will educate you on the risks of different withdrawal rates and the asset allocation that's appropriate for you. They should also help you select investments that have low costs and will perform well over the course of many years.

- To reduce the odds of error or fraud, arrange to have the monthly or quarterly withdrawals automatically deposited into your checking account.

Many 401(k) plans offer an installment payment feature that automatically makes monthly or quarterly payments to your checking account. You may want to use this installment feature if you like the investment funds in your employer's plan. Otherwise, you'll need to roll over your retirement savings to an IRA with better-performing funds. As of 2012, not many 401(k) plans offer managed payout funds, so you'll need to use an IRA rollover if you want to use a managed payout fund.

Common misconceptions

During the many retirement workshops I've held, I've often heard two common misconceptions about RIG #2:

Misconception #1: A withdrawal amount of 4% is safe.

Many people just automatically adopt a four percent withdrawal strategy, without thinking too hard about their own circumstances. When determining your withdrawal strategy, you absolutely must consider your longevity and, if applicable, that of your spouse or life partner. You can estimate your life expectancy, taking into account your family history and lifestyle, at www.livingto100.com or www.bluezones.com. (If you're doing the homework I've assigned you, this is Step #1.) Then once you have an idea of how long you might live, you can decide just how conservative or liberal you want to be with your withdrawal strategy. You'll also want to consider the expenses you'll have to pay to have someone manage your investments and to your financial advisor, if applicable. Finally, you'll want to take into account whether you can tolerate a reduction in your withdrawal amount if your retirement savings experience a significant downturn.

Misconception #2: I need access to my retirement savings. What if I need it for an emergency?

As with RIG #1 (investment income), financial planners often cite having access to your principal as a reason to use systematic withdrawals. But access to your savings is somewhat overrated. If you spend your savings, it won't be there anymore to generate a retirement paycheck! Although I think it's reasonable to have access to *some* of your retirement savings, you don't necessarily need to have access to *all* of your retirement savings.

Clearly there are differences and complexities in the way systematic withdrawals can work, and you'll need to spend some time learning about the different strategies and features that are possible. Don't simply choose the method or fund that generates the highest retirement income. Instead, do your homework with regards to your wants and needs – and your own specific circumstances – and then decide which funds will provide what you need.

I'm also not comfortable with a pure application of the four percent rule, where you lock in your withdrawal amount and continue it for the rest of your life. I'd prefer that you adjust your withdrawal amount to reflect your investment experience as it unfolds during your retirement and have a backup plan in place if you live a long time and need additional income. Chapter 7 goes into more detail regarding the adjustments and modifications to systematic withdrawals that I prefer you employ if you want to use this RIG.

The information in this chapter and the chapters that follow demonstrates that systematic withdrawals require the most ongoing attention of the three different ways to generate retirement income. If you just don't have the time, training, or patience to investigate the appropriate withdrawal rate and asset allocation for systematic withdrawals, either work with a trusted, qualified financial advisor (i.e. your "mechanic") or consider a more user-friendly RIG, such as investment income or immediate annuities. The consequences of making a mistake with systematic withdrawals are just too severe.

Part Two of this book details the other issues posed by systematic withdrawals, including refining your withdrawal rate, investment and tax considerations, and the IRS required minimum distribution (RMD).

CHAPTER 5

Retirement Income Generator #3: Immediate Annuities

Many people long for the days of traditional, employer-sponsored pension plans, where, after you retire, you're paid a monthly income for the rest of your life, no matter how long you live. Unfortunately, many of these plans have been discontinued. But don't give up hope! If you wish you had a plan this easy, I've got good news for you: You can create a "do it yourself" pension by buying an immediate annuity from an insurance company. With this retirement income-generating method, you hand over a portion of your retirement savings to an insurance company and it pays you a monthly benefit for the rest of your life.

Using the vehicle analogy I introduced earlier, an immediate annuity is like that basic, reliable sedan that keeps chugging along for years with no expensive maintenance or repairs. As with buying such a car, once you do your homework and purchase the right type of annuity, the monthly income will keep coming in with minimal effort on your part. Let's take a look to see how these work.

Basic varieties of immediate annuities

Before we delve into the details of retirement income generator (RIG) #3, I want to make it very clear that I'll be talking about *immediate* annuities and not *deferred variable* annuities. Deferred variable annuities are investment vehicles that can have high expenses and poor investment performance, are often sold by brokers, and are used for accumulating assets *before retirement.* They are a completely different animal from immediate annuities, whose primary purpose is to generate income *during your retirement.* I wanted to explain the difference from the get go because sometimes when people see the word "annuity," they jump to the conclusion that you're referring to deferred variable annuities.

Now let's discuss the three basic types of immediate annuities available to you. The first is an *immediate fixed* annuity, sometimes called a "single premium immediate annuity," or SPIA. With this type of annuity, your monthly income is fixed at a specific dollar amount. It's that simple – and that's really all you need to know.

The second basic type of immediate annuity is an *inflation-adjusted* annuity, in which your income is adjusted for inflation, usually as measured by the Consumer Price Index (CPI). This type of annuity will cost more than the fixed annuity described above, because you'll receive increases in your future retirement paychecks. An inflation-adjusted annuity neatly eliminates two significant risks that you face in retirement – the risk of inflation and the risk of outliving your retirement savings. An alternative to an inflation-adjusted annuity is one that's increased at a fixed rate, for example 3% per year, instead of the CPI; this type of annuity is typically a little less expensive than an inflation-adjusted annuity, and it can be a good substitute if you want protection against inflation.

The third basic type is an *immediate variable* annuity, where your monthly income is adjusted according to the performance of an underlying portfolio of stocks and bonds. This option offers a potential for income growth, but it exposes you to some market risk. That's because your monthly income is typically adjusted – up or down – to the extent that the performance of the underlying portfolio is different from an "assumed investment rate" or AIR. Typical AIRs are 3½%, 4%, or 5%. So if your variable annuity has an AIR of 4% per year and the underlying portfolio earns 6% during the year, your monthly income would be increased by about 2%. On the other hand, if the portfolio earns just 1% that year, your monthly income would be decreased by about 3%.

With any of the above types of immediate annuities, you have the ability to also protect your spouse or partner with a *joint and survivor* annuity, which pays a monthly income as long as either one of you is alive. You can specify the percentage of your income that's to be continued after your death to your spouse or partner; generally these percentages are 50, 66⅔, 75, or 100. This type of annuity will cost more than an annuity that covers just one person.

After purchasing a joint and survivor annuity, let's say you get worried that you and your spouse or partner might die unexpectedly soon after the annuity starts and the insurance company will "win" by getting to keep all your money. In this case, you can add a *period certain* option that guarantees that payments will be continued to another named beneficiary or to your estate for a specified period – typically five, 10, or 15 years.

Immediate annuity pros and cons

There are two drawbacks to buying the previous types of immediate annuities:

1. Once you buy the annuity, you can't change your mind and get your money back. You also can't access your money if you should need it in the event of an emergency.

2. When you and your beneficiary die, no money goes to your heirs.

These two drawbacks are the price you pay for the two significant advantages of an immediate annuity:

1. An immediate annuity usually generates the highest amount of initial retirement income, compared to the other two RIGs, investment income and systematic withdrawals.

2. Buying an immediate annuity guarantees that you won't outlive your money, and if you buy an inflation-adjusted annuity, you're also guaranteed protection against inflation.

Why can you get more lifetime income from an annuity? An insurance company looks at average life expectancies when they price immediate annuities for large groups of people – they can use the law of large numbers for pricing. But when you withdraw from your retirement savings with systematic withdrawals, you have to manage to the worst case, which is you living well beyond your life expectancy. And you need to manage to the law of one number – you! Living a long time might be a good thing, but it's a significant financial risk.

If you fully understand longevity risk and you use RIG #2 – systematic withdrawals – to generate retirement income, you should be extremely concerned about outliving your money. If you use systematic withdrawals, you'll need to be appropriately cautious and withdraw from your savings at a low rate. Successfully setting up systematic withdrawals so that you don't outlive your retirement savings usually means you'll die with money left over – money that you could have spent had you known exactly when you would die.

An annuity allows you (and the insurance company) to apply all your principal to generating retirement income without any money left over after you die. In essence, you "die broke" if you invest all your retirement savings in an annuity, but you won't be broke *before* you die, either. Of course, some people don't want to die broke because they want to leave money to their heirs or to charities. If these people can manage to live on just interest and dividends or very low withdrawals from their principal, then they might not need an immediate annuity.

An annuity has one more useful feature that's often overlooked: It's very user-friendly. You don't need to manage your investments, think about withdrawal rates, or work with financial planners – your annuity income is automatically deposited into your checking account each month. You may especially appreciate this when you get to your later years and are less interested in managing your investments, or are less able to focus on these types of decisions. Many people who develop dementia in their later years have lost all their savings due to mistakes or fraud, and an annuity neatly addresses this risk.

As you can see, there are trade-offs you have to make between the different types of RIGs, which is why I recommend that you not put all your retirement savings in an immediate annuity.

Hybrid varieties

There are other types of annuities that might be of interest to you, including these two:

Guaranteed lifetime withdrawal benefits (GLWB), also known as guaranteed minimum withdrawal benefits (GMWB). These products attempt to provide the best features of both systematic withdrawals and immediate annuities, and they address the drawbacks of the immediate annuities described above. With this type of annuity, you have the guarantee of a fixed lifetime income with the possibility of increases in your income if you achieve favorable investment returns, but with no downward adjustment for unfavorable investment returns. In addition, you can cancel the annuity and withdraw your savings at any time. Finally, any unused funds at your death can provide a financial legacy.

GLWB products can also be used to protect your retirement savings in the five to 10 years immediately prior to your retirement. Your savings might increase if your investments perform well, but your savings are guaranteed not to decrease if stock or bond markets drop.

But all these features come at a cost: In addition to the usual investment management fees, your retirement savings are assessed an annual insurance charge of 1% or more of your retirement savings, which can add up over the years. As a result, you'll most likely receive an income over your lifetime that's lower than what you'd get from a traditional fixed annuity, and your heirs will receive a lower legacy than if you had chosen to use a systematic withdrawal approach.

GLWBs are complex products, so it can be difficult to understand the contract provisions that adjust your income and calculate your surrender value. For example, you typically forfeit the insurance guarantees if you withdraw your savings.

As a result, you'll want to invest in a GLWB product only if you plan to stay with the product for the rest of your life. Despite their complications, these products can be appropriate in certain circumstances, since they do a good job of addressing some common objections people may have to buying annuities. If you'd like more details on GLWB/GMWB products, including shopping tips, see Chapter 16 in Part Two of this book.

Longevity insurance, a.k.a. advanced life deferred annuity (ALDA). This is an annuity that you buy when you retire but whose monthly income starts at an advanced age, say age 80 or 85. With the purest form of longevity insurance, if you die before the specified age, no benefits are payable. Other forms have a death benefit if you die before the specified age, but they cost more.

With longevity insurance, you can create a hybrid strategy that also provides the best features of systematic withdrawals and annuities. You can use systematic withdrawals to generate retirement income until the longevity insurance kicks in; the longevity insurance helps provide peace of mind that you won't outlive your savings. See Chapter 6 on hybrid strategies for more details on this approach.

How do immediate annuities meet the LIFE goals?

Depending on the type of annuity you choose, immediate annuities meet either two or three of the **LIFE** goals described in Chapter 2 (these results don't apply to the GLWB or longevity insurance products described previously):

- **Longevity protection:** ***Yes.*** You can't outlive your monthly income due to the insurance company guarantees.
- **Inflation protection:** ***Yes for inflation-adjusted annuities, no for fixed annuities, and maybe for variable annuities.*** With a variable annuity, you'll realize growth in your income only to the extent to which the underlying portfolio delivers good investment performance.
- **Flexibility and potential for a Financial legacy:** ***No.*** As noted above, most immediate annuities don't provide access to your savings, and there's usually no money left as a legacy for your children or charities.
- **Exposure to market risk is minimized:** ***Yes with fixed and inflation-adjusted annuities, no with variable annuities.*** Your monthly income with fixed and inflation-adjusted annuities isn't affected by stock market performance, but the monthly income from variable annuities fluctuates according to the performance of an underlying portfolio.

Note that immediate annuities have different **LIFE** ratings than RIG #1, investment income, and RIG #2, systematic withdrawals.

Retirement income scorecard

The retirement income generated from this RIG will vary depending on the type of annuity you purchase; it will also be affected by your age, sex, and marital status. To provide more of an across-the-board look at this method, I've included charts below that show the annual incomes for a standard fixed annuity, a variable annuity, a GLWB annuity, and an inflation-adjusted annuity. There are separate charts for a single man, a single woman, and a married couple with a 100% joint and survivor annuity at three different ages as of July 2012.

For fixed and inflation-adjusted annuities, I used rates from Vanguard's Annuity Access service that uses Hueler's Income Solutions platform. For GLWB annuities, I used withdrawal rates for Prudential's IncomeFlex annuity, which is available in many 401(k) plans. For variable annuities, I used rates from Vanguard's immediate variable annuity offered with American General Life Insurance Company, with an assumed investment return (AIR) of 3½%. These payout rates are not to be confused with investment rates of returns.

Figures 5.1, 5.2, and 5.3 will help you compare the annual payout rates of immediate annuities to the other methods of generating retirement income.

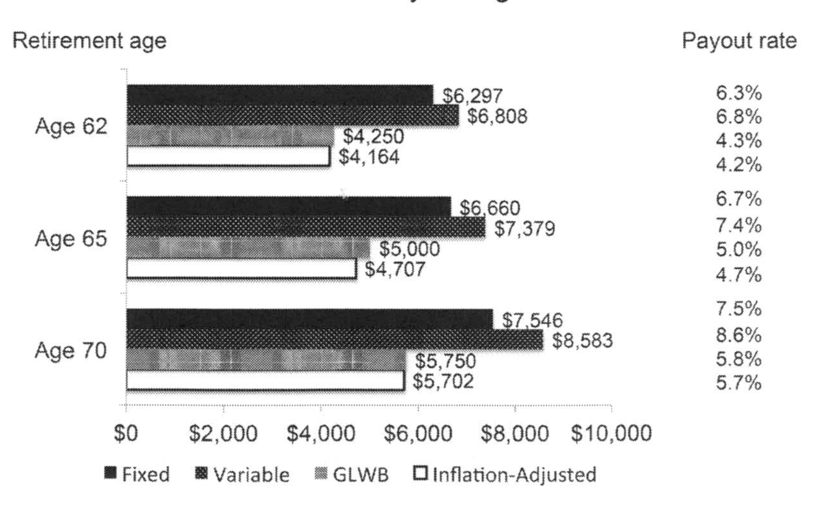

FIGURE 5.1 RETIREMENT INCOME SCORECARD: IMMEDIATE ANNUITIES, MEN

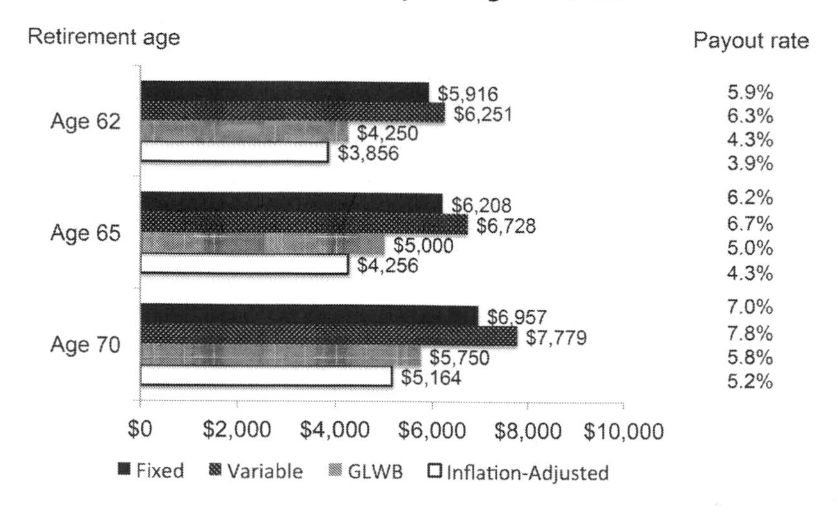

FIGURE 5.2 RETIREMENT INCOME SCORECARD: IMMEDIATE ANNUITIES, WOMEN

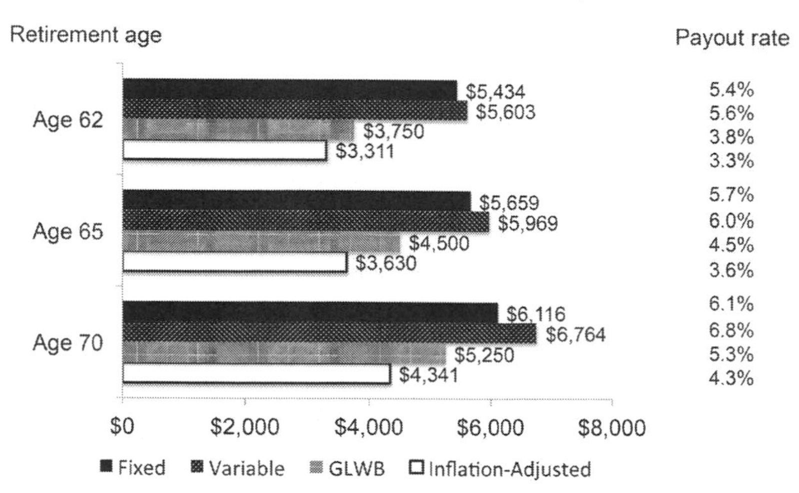

FIGURE 5.3 RETIREMENT INCOME SCORECARD: IMMEDIATE ANNUITIES, MARRIED COUPLE

It's interesting to note that the amount of retirement income you can generate at age 65 with an inflation-adjusted annuity is very close to the amount you can generate from RIG #2 – systematic withdrawals – using the four percent rule for determining your withdrawal amounts. But keep in mind that with an inflation-adjusted annuity, you're *guaranteed* a lifetime income that increases for inflation. With systematic withdrawals, there are no guarantees – how long you live and your investment experience will dictate whether you'll meet your financial goals. And the four percent rule has been questioned lately as being too high, given the current low interest rate environment.

Money for LIFE™ goals and amount of retirement income

Figure 5.4 shows a convenient summary of how three basic types of immediate annuities meet the **LIFE** goals and the initial amount of retirement income that's possible, for the purposes of comparing this method to other RIGs.

Goal	Immediate fixed annuity	Immediate inflation-adjusted annuity	Immediate variable annuity
Amount of initial income	●	○	●
Longevity protection	●	●	●
Inflation protection	○	●	◑
Flexibility and Financial legacy	○	○	○
Exposure is minimized	●	●	○

● = high or strong
◑ = medium or maybe
○ = low or none

FIGURE 5.4 LIFE GOAL RANKING FOR IMMEDIATE ANNUITIES

Figure 5.5 shows the same summary for the hybrid varieties of annuities.

Goal	GLWB/GMWB	Longevity annuity w/sys withdrawals
Amount of initial income	◐	◐
Longevity protection	●	◐
Inflation protection	◐	◐
Flexibility and Financial legacy	◐	◐
Exposure is minimized	●	◐

● = high or strong
◐ = medium or maybe
○ = low or none

FIGURE 5.5 LIFE GOAL RANKING FOR HYBRID ANNUITIES

Shopping tips

Here are my five tips for buying an annuity that best fits your needs:

1. Be sure to shop around. There are many highly rated insurance companies that offer immediate fixed or inflation-adjusted annuities. At any point in time, one or two might be offering more monthly income for your investment dollars than the other companies due to their own capacity or marketing strategies. Before purchasing an annuity, get quotes from five or more insurance companies, and be sure you're making an apples-to-apples comparison of the same type of annuity.

2. Only purchase an annuity from a highly rated company. Because you can't outlive your annuity income, an immediate annuity is really the safest part of your retirement income. But to help insure your money's safety, I'd suggest only investigating insurance companies that have earned the highest three or four ratings from the rating agencies, such as A.M. Best or Standard & Poor's.

3. Don't make things too complicated by adding on riders you don't need. Resist convincing arguments from insurance agents to add costly riders to your annuity, such as coupling your annuity with life insurance or long-term care insurance. These just make it more difficult to comparison shop, and they add to the cost of your annuity.

4. Understand the treatment of sales commissions. Commissions come right out of your investment, so a higher commission to the agent means less monthly income for you. The best way to deal with this is to make sure that the amount of the monthly income quoted is what you'll get after sales commissions have been paid, so that your comparison-shopping takes the commission level into account. Whether you're working with an insurance agent or a shopping service, be sure to ask about the commissions. If you can't get a straight answer, move on.

5. Consider diversifying by purchasing more than one annuity from different companies. You might want to think about spreading your annuity purchase among two or three insurance companies in order to reduce your exposure to insurance company bankruptcy. For example, suppose you have $300,000 to invest in an annuity. For each insurance company you investigate, get quotes on investing $100,000, $200,000, and $300,000. If you spread your investment among two or three companies, your total income might not be much less than investing with just one company and you'll have more peace of mind. Chapter 15 in Part Two of this book offers more thoughts on bankruptcy protection.

All this investigating may sound like a lot of work, and it is, which is why you're probably much better off using an online shopping service such as Vanguard's Annuity Access program that uses the Hueler Income Solutions platform. This platform is also available through many 401(k) plans, and has telephone representatives who will answer your questions and discuss the suitability of an annuity for you. Another popular online shopping service is ImmediateAnnuities.com.

There are a number of benefits to using an online annuity shopping service as opposed to working with an individual insurance agent, including these:

- You can bid your annuity among several insurance companies to obtain the lowest price.
- You can see the safety ratings of all the companies in one place.
- Commission costs should be transparent so you can compare what you'll be paying to each company.
- You can easily vary the amount of your investment with each insurance company to help you analyze the benefit of diversification.

- There's no agent trying to talk you into costly riders.

You can buy fixed or inflation-adjusted annuities at either of the above-mentioned annuity shopping services. If you're interested in variable annuities, one source with low fees and above-average investment performance is Vanguard, which offers an immediate variable annuity in which your monthly income is adjusted by the underlying performance of a Vanguard mutual fund. After you purchase your annuity, you're allowed to change the mutual fund that adjusts your income if you decide to change your investment goals. This flexibility and the low fees differentiate the Vanguard product from other variable annuities.

As mentioned previously, some 401(k) and other employer-sponsored plans have one or more type of annuities in their plans – fixed, inflation-adjusted, or GLWB. Many other plans don't offer any annuity options. In this case, if you want an annuity, you'll need to roll over your accounts to an IRA at a financial institution that has the annuities you want.

Even if your 401(k) plan offers an annuity, it's possible you could get a better annuity deal with another financial institution. In order to evaluate your options, it pays to compare the amount and type of annuity in your employer's plan to annuities available through an IRA rollover to a financial institution.

Common misconceptions

Throughout the many years I've worked as an actuary and a retirement expert, I've heard many common misconceptions about investing in an immediate annuity to generate a lifetime income. Some of these misconceptions are perpetuated by financial advisors who have expertise and training in investments, and who are more comfortable with an investing approach as compared to an insurance approach. They tend to "short sell" and even criticize immediate annuities, but their critiques can be misleading. A more cynical reason for their misleading comments is that these financial advisors won't earn any ongoing advisory fees once the annuity has been purchased. Of course, there are many financial advisors who will explain the pros and cons of both annuities and systematic withdrawals, and will help you make the best decision for your goals and circumstances.

There are also many annuity products out there that are very confusing and complex, such as deferred variable annuities or certain GLWB/GMWB retail products. These products often earn high commissions for agents or have high profit loads, which can generate hostility toward *all* types of annuities. The simple, immediate annuities that I prefer can get disregarded if they're lumped in with these undesirable annuities.

Don't throw the baby out with the bath water.

That being said, let's address some of the common misconceptions you might hear during your investigation:

Misconception #1: If I die early in my retirement, the insurance company wins. I don't want the insurance company to win!

Actually, the real winners are the other annuity policyholders who live well beyond their life expectancies. The retirement paychecks for these lucky people are funded with the premiums paid by people who die before the life expectancy estimated by the insurance company. In a sense, the people who die young are "paying it forward" to those who live longer. Insurance companies take this into account when they price annuities, and they act as the intermediary for insuring the financial security of the entire group of annuity holders who are "all in this together."

Misconception #2: Interest rates are low right now, so it's a bad time to buy an annuity.

Yes, it's true that interest rates are low in 2012; if interest rates rise, annuity costs will drop. That's because the insurance company will earn more money if interest rates rise, so they can charge less for an annuity. But it's also true that if you invest in bonds in 2012, you'll also earn a very low interest rate. The fact is, the relative comparison between buying an annuity and investing in bonds hasn't changed – both approaches produce a lower retirement paycheck in a low interest rate environment. It's basically an expensive time to retire.

Misconception #3: I don't want to pay profits to an insurance company for the rest of my life.

Everybody hates the big, bad insurance companies! The reality is, you've got to pay profits to somebody, no matter what you do. If you don't buy an annuity from an insurance company, then you'll be paying profits to your financial advisor, the mutual fund company, or some other financial institution that invests your money.

I fully understand the frustration people have with insurance companies, particularly when it comes to the fine print in medical insurance policies. But you can find immediate annuities that are competitively priced with a minimum of confusing fine print. As with anything else, there are good and bad annuities, just as there are good and bad financial advisors and good and bad mutual funds. Your job is to find the product that works best for you.

Misconception #4: I won't have access to my savings. What if I need it for an emergency?

Yes, that's true with the type of annuities that I prefer. And that's why I wouldn't suggest you put all your retirement savings into an annuity. I'd limit your annuity to half of your savings at the beginning of your retirement and maybe as much as two-thirds or three-quarters as you get older and are less able to manage your investments. And it's always a good idea to set aside a liquid reserve for emergencies.

But access to your savings is overrated, as I've noted in Chapters 3 and 4. Remember, if you can access your savings and you spend it, the money's no longer generating retirement income for you.

In spite of these considerations, if having access to your savings is your primary obstacle to buying an annuity, then consider a GLWB/GMWB product that gives you access to your savings – but at a cost.

Misconception #5: What if the insurance company goes bankrupt, like AIG did? I'll lose all my money!

As I note in Chapter 15, state insurance guaranty associations will protect your annuity policy in the event of the insurance company's bankruptcy, subject to certain limits. To address this risk, you should only buy annuities from the highest-rated insurance companies and keep your purchases below the limits of your state's guaranty fund.

By the way, the life insurance subsidiary of AIG that sold annuities didn't go bankrupt. The assets backing its annuity policies were protected from creditors, and annuity policyholders never needed the protection of the state insurance guaranty associations.

Misconception #6: My retirement paycheck will be fixed and will be ravaged by inflation. In a few years, I won't be able to buy a bag of groceries.

If you buy a fixed annuity and experience high inflation, this criticism is correct. But you'll have the same problem if you invest in most bonds. On the other hand, if you experience low inflation and if your spending declines during your retirement, inflation is less of a concern. If you're really worried about inflation, buy an inflation-adjusted annuity or an annuity that increases at a fixed rate, such as 3%.

Once again, this is a reason to diversify your retirement income by investing part of your retirement savings to protect against inflation and the other part for certainty and the guarantee of a paycheck for the rest of your life.

Misconception #7: Once I buy the annuity, my money is gone.

Yes, but this is a perceptual challenge. For instance, if you have $300,000 in retirement savings and use $140,000 to buy an annuity, all that's left in your investments is $160,000. You might feel poorer by $140,000 because you can't see it or access it anymore. But think about when you were working for a salary. Most likely, you were paid several hundred thousand dollars or even a million or two over your decades of work. Did you feel poorer because you didn't have access to all this money at the beginning of your career? No, because all that really counted was your monthly paycheck.

You might think from my responses to these misconceptions that I work for an insurance company. Actually, I've never worked for an insurance company – I've always worked at independent consulting firms or had my own retirement education business. But my years of professional training as an actuary help me assess and analyze the risk of living too long, and I believe that the right kind of annuity is a good tool to address this risk.

This chapter has explained the basics of immediate annuities so that you can understand the next chapters that describe hybrid strategies and my five favorite ways of generating retirement income. There is more you may want to learn about buying annuities, such as the tax treatment, more details on the other varieties and strategies mentioned above, and how to protect yourself against the bankruptcy of your insurance company. You'll find more on those topics in Part Two.

CHAPTER 6

Hybrid Solutions

While some people will find it easy to choose between the three retirement income generators (RIGs) in order to generate a monthly paycheck from their retirement savings, others may find it difficult to determine the best solution. That may be because they believe that all of the **LIFE** goals are important to them or because they find it hard to choose between the "control vs. certainty" tradeoff I described in Chapter 2.

If you think you may have a hard time making a choice among the three RIGs, then you're a good candidate for a hybrid strategy that combines two or more of the RIGs. This chapter describes some of the common hybrid strategies and how you might apply them to your circumstances. Chapters 8 and 9 outline a more formal process for deciding which RIG, or combination of RIGs, might be best for your goals and circumstances; that process can also be used to select one of the hybrid solutions described in this chapter.

Applying the vehicle analogy I introduced previously, using two or more RIGs is like the family that owns two very different cars, such as a sporty coupe and a minivan, that meet varying transportation needs. Let's start with the simplest hybrid solutions, then we'll get more complex.

Split your retirement savings

The simplest hybrid solution is to split your savings between two or more RIGs, so that you can realize the advantages of each type. For example, you could split your retirement savings 50/50 between investing – either RIG #1 (investment income) or RIG #2 (systematic withdrawals) – and an immediate annuity, RIG #3. This gives you control and access to the portion of your savings invested in one of the first two RIGS and the guarantee of a lifetime income from the immediate annuity.

If you choose this strategy, you will still need to make the necessary decisions for each type of RIG. For instance, for the portion of your retirement savings that you devote to systematic withdrawals, you'll need to determine the withdrawal rate and asset allocation. For the portion of your retirement savings that you devote to immediate annuities, you'll need to choose between fixed, inflation-adjusted, variable, or GLWB annuities.

There's no set formula for deciding how you might best split your retirement savings between each type of RIG. One possibility is to cover your required basic living expenses with a fixed or inflation-adjusted annuity, and then cover the rest of your discretionary living expenses with investment income or systematic withdrawals. This way, even if your investments do poorly or you live well past your life expectancy, your basic living expenses will still be covered. Some financial advisors call this approach "building a floor and then exposing to the upside."

Another possible strategy would be to decide how much of your retirement savings you want to leave as a legacy for your children or charities, and then use RIG #1 (investment income) for this chunk of your retirement savings. Then you can devote the remainder of your savings to an immediate annuity, so you have the guarantee of a lifetime retirement paycheck.

Or you could simply split your savings by some other proportion that might feel right to you, such as 50/50, 25/75, or 75/25.

Phased annuity purchase

Many people feel uncertain about a number of factors at the beginning of their retirement. For example, you may not know if you'll like being retired and decide to work part time, or you might not have decided yet where you'll live. If you're married, maybe one of you will want to continue working but for an uncertain period of time. In any of these situations, it's understandable that you may be unwilling to give up control of most of your retirement savings to purchase an annuity from an insurance company.

In this case, another simple hybrid strategy is to start your retirement with a modest portion of your savings, say one-fourth, devoted to an immediate annuity, and then invest the rest of your savings for investment income or systematic withdrawals. This way, you start your retirement maintaining control and flexibility over the bulk of your retirement savings.

As you age, you'll probably settle into your spending routines and may be more willing to give up control of your retirement savings in exchange for the certainty that immediate annuities offer. Or you may become less interested or less able to continue monitoring your investments and the withdrawal percentage you get from systematic withdrawals. Periodically, say every five or 10 years, you might take a significant chunk of your remaining retirement savings and buy another immediate annuity. One advantage to this strategy is that you can diversify your annuity purchases between a few different insurance companies to address the risk of insurance company bankruptcy.

Another advantage is that annuities get cheaper as you age, since the insurance company expects to pay your retirement income for a shorter period of time. You can see how this works by looking at the retirement income scorecards in Chapter 5. For example, $100,000 buys an inflation-adjusted, 100% joint and survivor annuity for a married couple that generates $3,311 per year at age 62, $3,630 per year at age 65, and $4,341 per year at age 70.

Once again, there's no set formula for deciding how often you might buy another immediate annuity or how much of your remaining savings you might devote to buying that annuity. When it comes to investing in annuities, it really depends on your circumstances and your comfort level. For instance, one common situation I've seen occurs when one partner – often the husband – is the person who manages the finances, and that person is older than the other partner, often the wife. As the husband ages, he can make sure his wife's finances will be secure after he passes away by devoting a larger portion of their retirement savings to an annuity.

Systematic withdrawals with longevity insurance

Some people might prefer the flexibility and access that systematic withdrawals offer but feel uneasy about the prospect of outliving their retirement savings. If this sounds like you, you can use systematic withdrawals to generate retirement income until a specified advanced age, for example, age 80 or 85. You'd dedicate most of your retirement savings to this purpose and design your withdrawal strategy so that this portion of your savings is exhausted when you attain the specified advanced age.

With the smaller portion of your retirement savings, you'd buy an annuity that starts a lifetime retirement paycheck at that advanced age. A married couple or committed partners could purchase a joint and survivor annuity so that both partners would be protected for life. If you like this solution and decide to implement it, you'll want to take into account how much retirement income you'll need at the advanced age, reflecting anticipated inflation and the possible need for long-term care.

This hybrid solution has the advantage of increasing the amount of your savings that you have control over, while still guaranteeing that you won't run out of money before you die. It also offers the potential for leaving a legacy if you die before the advanced age.

There are two different ways you can implement this strategy: true longevity insurance and the longevity reserve method. Let me explain how they work.

Method #1: True longevity insurance. When you retire, you can use a portion of your savings to buy an annuity that's delayed and doesn't start until you attain a pre-determined advanced age. This type of annuity is commonly called "longevity insurance" – insurance against the risk that you'll live too long! It may also be called a "longevity annuity." The portion of your retirement savings that you'd devote to buying longevity insurance can range from 15% to 33% of your retirement savings when you retire, depending on the age at which you start the annuity and whether the annuity has a death benefit.

The cheapest form of longevity insurance has no death benefit if you die before the advanced age. In this case, the insurance company uses the premium you paid to fund the retirement incomes of other policyholders who make it to the advanced age; this is an extreme example of the "pay it forward" feature of an annuity (see the misconceptions section in Chapter 5 for more details on this). You'd use this type of longevity insurance if you want to maximize your retirement income and don't mind "paying forward" the longevity insurance premium. Many people feel uncomfortable not getting a death benefit, however, so they're willing to pay a higher premium for longevity insurance that pays a benefit to your beneficiary if you die before the advanced age.

In 2012, two companies that offer longevity insurance include New York Life Insurance Co. and Fidelity Investments.

The financial institution UBS also offers their Lifetime Income solution to 401(k) plans. With this solution, during the years leading up to your retirement, a portion of your savings is used to buy an annuity that starts at age 80. The remainder of your savings is invested in a target date fund and is systematically withdrawn with the goal of using it up by age 80.

Method #2: Longevity reserve. At the beginning of your retirement, you would set aside and invest a portion of your retirement savings for a reserve that would buy an annuity at a pre-determined advanced age. You'd leave this amount invested and wouldn't draw from it for retirement income. The portion of your retirement savings that you devote to this reserve also typically ranges from 15% to 33% of your retirement savings at the time you retire, although it will most likely be higher than the cost of buying longevity insurance when you retire. The remainder of your savings would be invested and withdrawn with the intention that this savings would be exhausted at the age the annuity starts. With this reserve method, you wouldn't purchase the annuity until you reach the advanced age.

One advantage of this method is that if you die before the advanced age, the reserve can serve as a legacy for your children or charities.

This reserve method is offered in many 401(k) plans from the financial advisor company Financial Engines. With this solution, the reserve is typically applied to buy an annuity at age 85, although there is flexibility in applying the reserve.

Figure 6.1 shows a summary of how the Financial Engines Income + and UBS Lifetime Income solutions meet the **LIFE** goals.

Goal	Financial Engines Income +	UBS Lifetime Income
Amount of initial income	○	◑
Longevity protection	◑	●
Inflation protection	◑	◑
Flexibility and Financial legacy	●	◑
Exposure is minimized	◑	◑

● = high or strong
◑ = medium or maybe
○ = low or none

FIGURE 6.1 LIFE GOAL RANKING FOR TWO HYBRID SOLUTIONS

Whether you use true longevity insurance or the reserve method, it's likely that you might need the help of a financial advisor to decide exactly how much you should devote to either solution, and how to invest and draw down the remainder of your retirement savings. Be aware that this is one method of generating a retirement paycheck that might not lend itself well to "do it yourselfers."

But you can get help with implementing this solution. For example, if you're working with a company such as Financial Engines, you'll get help with the decisions mentioned above by noncommissioned telephone representatives, plus ongoing monitoring of your investments and drawdown amounts until you reach the advanced age. If the UBS solution is offered in your 401(k) plan, typically your 401(k) plan's administrators are trained to answer your questions.

One possibility for "do it yourselfers" is to use one of Fidelity's income replacement funds, which are intended to pay a retirement income until the specified target year, as described in Chapter 4. Then you would combine that fund with longevity insurance that starts the monthly income at the specified target year.

I happen to like the hybrid retirement solutions described in this chapter, since they diversify your retirement income – a strategy I'll discuss more in Chapter 8 – and can satisfy the greatest number of **LIFE** goals.

Now that you've learned the basics about the three RIGs, the next four chapters will help you design a retirement income solution that works best for your goals and life circumstances.

CHAPTER 7

My Five Favorite Retirement Paycheck Solutions

"C'mon, you're the expert. Just tell me what to do!"

I sometimes get this call for help from people who are frustrated by the time and effort it takes to analyze the different ways they can generate a retirement paycheck. And I tell them all the same thing:

"Hang in there! It's worth the effort."

Because we're dealing with a very critical part of your future, I strongly advocate that you take the time to seriously consider the retirement and financial goals that are important to you, and then shop for the retirement income generators (RIGs) that best fit your circumstances.

But because I also understand how hard it can be to do the necessary research, I'll meet you half-way and describe my five favorite solutions for generating a retirement paycheck. Each solution has its unique features, advantages, and disadvantages, and each generates a different amount of retirement income. Your specific objectives with respect to the **LIFE** goals described in Chapter 2 will influence which of these solutions might work best for you.

As you're reviewing these solutions, think of them as starting points for developing your own retirement income strategies – you needn't follow them to the letter. There can be good reasons for modifying these suggestions, and Part Two of this book describes more considerations to help you fine-tune your strategies. These five suggestions are simply intended to help you decide which retirement paycheck solution might work best for you.

If I knew nothing about your goals and circumstances, I'd suggest the first solution, which combines systematic withdrawals with immediate annuities, because it could work for just about anyone. Otherwise, I really don't prefer one solution over the others – any of these methods might be appropriate for you, given your goals and life circumstances. For each of the solutions, I describe the reasons why you might pick that solution. Lastly, please don't place any importance on the order in which these solutions appear – I didn't rank them from best to worst.

Solution #1: Split your retirement paycheck between systematic withdrawals and an immediate annuity.

If you divide your retirement savings between RIG #2 (systematic withdrawals) and RIG #3 (an immediate annuity), you'll realize the advantages of each while mitigating the disadvantages of both. The annuity will provide a paycheck that's guaranteed to last the rest of your life, and the systematic withdrawals method offers flexibility and access to a portion of your retirement savings.

What's the appropriate split between the annuity and the money you invest for systematic withdrawals? One effective approach, often referred to as the "income floor approach," is to estimate your essential, routine living costs, such as food, utilities, housing, property taxes, insurance premiums, and so on. Then buy an immediate annuity that produces enough income to cover these expenses. As long as the amount of your basic living expenses doesn't change, this method guarantees that they'll be covered for the rest of your life, no matter how long you live. If you're married or are in a committed relationship, be sure to cover your spouse or partner with a joint and survivor annuity.

With the remainder of your retirement savings, use RIG #2 (systematic withdrawals) to generate a retirement paycheck that will cover your discretionary expenses, such as vacations, entertainment, meals out, gifts, and so on.

To determine your initial annual withdrawal amount, use one of the three methods and the respective online systems described in Chapter 14. Then adjust your withdrawal amount every year or two, to reflect investment performance as it unfolds. Once you reach age 70½, you can also use the required minimum distribution (RMD) rules as guidelines for your annual withdrawal amount (see Chapter 12 for details on these rules).

Since you've covered your basic living expenses with the immediate annuity, you might be able to start with an initial withdrawal rate for RIG #2 that's a little higher than if you had used systematic withdrawals for *all* your retirement income, as described in Solution #2. If a stock market crash requires you to cut back on your withdrawals, using this method means you won't need to make drastic changes in your life, like going back to work or moving in with your kids, because you'll still have your essential living costs covered by the annuity.

One quick note: Even if you like this solution and expect you may use it, you'll still want to read about Solution #2, since it contains more details on implementing the systematic withdrawals method. Chapters 4 and 14 also outline the considerations for determining your withdrawal rate for systematic withdrawals.

For the immediate annuity that covers your basic living expenses, purchase an inflation-adjusted annuity if you want to be certain that inflation won't erode the value of your retirement paycheck. Be aware, however, that an inflation-adjusted annuity has a higher cost than an immediate fixed annuity. You could purchase a fixed annuity if you think your basic living expenses might not increase due to inflation, though that's a risky assumption in my opinion.

One other viable possibility is to use a guaranteed lifetime withdrawal benefit (GLWB) product for your guaranteed floor of lifetime income. This type of product gives you some potential for growth in your retirement income if your investments perform well, but it also assures that your income will never decrease if markets tank. The initial amount of retirement income you'll receive falls somewhere between the initial amounts you'd get with fixed annuities and inflation-adjusted annuities. Most likely your income from a GLWB product won't increase enough to keep pace with inflation, but there's a good chance you'll see some increases in your retirement income. If you're interested in this option, see Chapter 16 for more details on GLWB products.

An alternative to the floor income approach is to use a split between systematic withdrawals and an immediate annuity that you feel most comfortable with, such as a 50/50 split or a one-third/two-thirds split. Yet another approach to dividing your retirement paycheck between systematic withdrawals and an immediate annuity is to phase in your purchase of immediate annuities. In this case, you'd start your retirement with a low portion of your savings, say 25%, devoted to annuities. After several years, you'd buy an additional annuity with another portion of your retirement savings; this "hands off" RIG may be beneficial as you get older, when you may have less time or ability to monitor your investment and withdrawal strategies with systematic withdrawals.

As I stated at the beginning of this chapter, the combination of an immediate annuity and systematic withdrawals is the solution I'd suggest if I knew nothing about you. It combines the best features of systematic withdrawals and immediate annuities while mitigating the disadvantages of each. It can be reasonably implemented by do-it-yourselfers or with moderate involvement from a financial planner. And it produces a "Goldilocks" retirement paycheck that's not too high and not too low, compared to the other RIGs.

Solution #2: Choose systematic withdrawals with adjustments, a backup plan, and an investment strategy that protects against downturns.

RIG #2 (systematic withdrawals) might be most appropriate for you if you need a higher paycheck than provided by RIG #1 (investment income) and you're just absolutely opposed to buying any type of annuity from an insurance company. Some people really don't like to deal with insurance companies. While I don't agree with this position, I acknowledge that there are many people who might feel this way. If that's the case with you, you'll need to deal with the complexities of systematic withdrawals.

But I'm not comfortable recommending that you only use a pure application of systematic withdrawals, where you set your withdrawal amount when you retire, increase it for inflation each year, and never make mid-course adjustments. Instead, I recommend that you adopt the strategies discussed below.

Start with an annual withdrawal rate that has a low chance of failure, say one out of 10 or less. Unless you're confident of your abilities to understand the issues and make a decision on your own, I'd encourage you to work with a financial advisor who's been trained in withdrawal strategies to help you determine your rate of withdrawal.

If you decide to go it alone, be sure to read Chapter 14, which goes into more detail on determining safe withdrawal rates, and learn more from articles by qualified analysts; Dr. Wade Pfau's *Retirement Researcher* blog is a good place to start. You can also use online software that can help you determine the withdrawal rate that's appropriate for you (Chapter 14 also provides information on software that's available). And don't just do what everybody else is doing – for instance, choosing a 4% withdrawal rate just because you heard your best friend is doing that. Instead, do your homework to determine a withdrawal rate that works best with your needs and circumstances.

You might want to use a lower initial withdrawal amount than what I suggested in Solution #1 above, because you'll be completely relying on your retirement savings to generate your retirement paycheck. The consequences of failure are higher when you rely exclusively on systematic withdrawals, so you'll want to be more cautious with your withdrawal strategy.

You'll also want to plan to periodically adjust your withdrawals up or down to reflect the performance of your investments as they unfold over your retirement.

In addition, you'll want to have a backup plan in place should you need to reduce your withdrawals due to a market downturn early in your retirement. That backup plan could involve reducing your living expenses, going back to work, tapping into other assets, or moving in with your kids.

And here's one more detail: You should adopt an investment strategy that will protect you from having to sell some of your savings at a market bottom or prevent you from panic selling.

Sound complicated? Let's go into more detail about making mid-course adjustments in your withdrawal amounts and investment strategies to protect against market downturns to make this solution a little easier to understand.

During your first year of retirement, set your annual retirement paycheck equal to your withdrawal rate multiplied by the amount of your retirement savings at the beginning of the year. Then every year or two thereafter, adjust your retirement paycheck by reapplying the withdrawal percentage to the amount of your retirement savings remaining at that time. This way, you can adjust your retirement paycheck up or down to reflect your investment experience as it unfolds during your retirement.

When you reach your 70s, revisit your withdrawal rate again; you might be able to increase it to reflect the fewer years you have left to live. Then revisit it once more when you get to your 80s or if you experience a significant life event such as the death of a spouse or a significant long-term care need.

If your retirement savings are in tax-advantaged retirement accounts, such as traditional IRAs, or deductible or Roth 401(k) accounts, once you reach age 70½, you'll need to withdraw enough money to comply with the IRS rules on required minimum distributions (RMD). These rules spread your withdrawals over your remaining expected lifetime and can serve as reasonable guidelines for an appropriate withdrawal amount. (Chapter 12 provides details on the RMD rules.) Note that these rules don't apply to Roth IRAs or ordinary investment accounts that don't have special tax advantages, though you could still use these rules as guidance for your withdrawal amounts.

In addition to the above suggestions, I'd also encourage you to revisit your withdrawal rate any time there's a "shock" to your retirement savings due to a market downturn. One possible threshold is if your savings decline by more than 15% since you last set your withdrawal amount. And if you're not sure what the appropriate threshold should be, I'd recommend that you consult a financial advisor.

Here are some key details that will help you successfully implement this investment strategy:

- Invest in a balanced or target date mutual fund with very low fees, such as the Fidelity, T. Rowe Price, or Vanguard funds mentioned in Chapter 3, or index funds that have very low expenses (below 50 basis points, or 0.50%), such as funds from Fidelity, Schwab, or Vanguard. I suggest you keep your asset allocation between one-third stocks/two-thirds bonds and two-thirds stocks/one-third bonds. This range offers some potential for growth in your savings while providing some protection against market volatility. If you're not comfortable choosing your asset allocation, you may want to work with a financial advisor to help you determine what's best for you.

- If you can't tolerate much of a downward adjustment in your withdrawal amount due to a stock market downturn because you're living "close to the edge," keep your allocation to equities at the lower end of the asset allocation range.

- If you feel comfortable taking some risks or if you can tolerate lowering your withdrawal amounts due to a stock market downturn, you might consider an allocation to stocks that's near the higher end of the range discussed above.

- Adopt an investment strategy that will prevent you from needing to sell your stock investments during a downturn. One technique is to always keep two or three years' worth of principal withdrawals in safe, liquid investments.

- A more sophisticated strategy to accomplish this objective (not being forced to sell your investments) would be to use the bucket approach or age-banding I described in Chapter 4. Most likely, you'll need to work with a financial planner to carry out this strategy.

- As much as possible, use low-cost index funds and rebalance your portfolio periodically to match your asset allocation goals.

If this sounds like a lot of work and you're discouraged by the amount of effort involved, you have two choices: Either work with a trusted, qualified financial advisor or consider another retirement paycheck solution. If you decide to work with a financial advisor, Chapter 11 offers some considerations for choosing a qualified advisor.

Solution #3: Use systematic withdrawals combined with longevity insurance or a longevity reserve.

This approach provides the flexibility of systematic withdrawals during the first 10 to 20 years of your retirement, with the guarantee of a lifetime income in case you live well beyond your life expectancy. Here's how it works.

You'll use systematic withdrawals to generate your retirement paycheck up to an advanced age; ages 80 or 85 are typical ages for this purpose. Then, you'll use a lifetime annuity to generate your retirement paycheck after that age. At the start of your retirement, you'll take one of the following steps to make sure you'll have this lifetime annuity when you reach the advanced age:

1. When you retire, you'll buy an annuity that will start at your specified advanced age (if you live that long). This type of annuity goes by a few different names: "longevity annuity" or "longevity insurance" are most common. The cheapest form of longevity insurance doesn't pay any benefit if you die before the advanced age (remember the "pay it forward" concept from Chapter 5). More expensive versions will have a partial death benefit if you die before the advanced age.

2. You'll set aside a reserve that will grow with investment earnings and is projected to be sufficient to buy an immediate annuity when you reach the advanced age. Don't withdraw from this reserve before you reach the advanced age. If you don't live to this age, the money can serve as a legacy to your children or charities. The amount of this reserve should range from 15% to 33% of your retirement savings at the beginning of your retirement, depending on whether the annuity starts at age 80 or 85.

With this solution, you'll plan your withdrawals in such a way that the amount of your retirement savings devoted to systematic withdrawals will be exhausted by the time you reach the advanced age. It's important to point out that you don't need to use the periodic adjustments and backup plan I described for Solution #2 for your systematic withdrawals, since you have the annuity as a backup that will start if you live to the advanced age.

There's a good chance you'll need to work with a financial advisor to implement this retirement paycheck solution. An advisor can help you with the necessary steps, which include purchasing the longevity insurance or determining the amount of the longevity reserve, investing your retirement savings, and determining the safest withdrawal amounts until you reach the advanced age.

The first method of this solution described above – using longevity insurance – is the method used by the financial institution UBS, and may be offered in some 401(k) plans. With their approach, systematic withdrawals are used to generate a retirement paycheck until age 80; after this age, the annuity provides a guaranteed lifetime paycheck.

The second variation of this solution described above – the reserve method – is the method used by the financial advising company Financial Engines, which is offered by many 401(k) plans. Financial Engines has both online software and telephone representatives that can help you with the decisions I mentioned above. They'll also help you make mid-course adjustments, if necessary, and will assist you with the annuity purchase when you reach the advanced age. Financial Engines charges for this service; their fee ranges from 0.20% to 0.60% (20 to 60 basis points) of your retirement savings, depending on their arrangement with the 401(k) plan.

When this book was written, the Financial Engines and UBS solutions were only available through employer-sponsored plans, such as 401(k) plans, and are not available to individuals on their own.

You might be able to implement this solution yourself, using products designed for this purpose. For example, you could use one of the Fidelity income replacement funds that are intended to be exhausted by the target date, and buy longevity insurance to kick in after that date. Chapter 4 describes Fidelity's income replacement funds in more detail.

Solution #4: Purchase immediate annuities.

I'd encourage you to devote a significant amount of your retirement savings to immediate annuities if one or more of the following circumstances applies to you:

- you want the highest amount of initial retirement income,
- you aren't concerned about leaving a legacy with your retirement funds,
- you want the simplicity of a retirement paycheck that's on auto-pilot so you don't have to lift a finger once you initially establish it, or
- you don't want there to be any possibility that you'll outlive your retirement paycheck.

If any of these goals apply to you, I'd choose this method, though I wouldn't recommend devoting *all* of your retirement savings to an immediate annuity. You should still have some retirement savings set aside that you can access if needs arise. One possibility that would cover this would be to devote one-third of your savings to an immediate fixed annuity, one-third to an immediate variable annuity, and one-third to RIG #1 (investment income). Another possibility is to use a GLWB product for two-thirds of your savings, and RIG #1 for the remaining third.

The use of RIG #1 for one-third of your savings means you'll hold this amount of principal in reserve in case you want to increase withdrawals in the future to adjust for inflation. Or if you want more protection against inflation, you can use an inflation-adjusted annuity – instead of a fixed or variable annuity – for one-third of your retirement savings.

Solution #5: Use just interest and dividends.

This solution is a pure application of RIG #1 – using the money you'll get from just interest and dividends to pay for your retirement living expenses. You can make this solution easy by investing in a low-cost mutual fund that's balanced between stocks and bonds and having the dividends deposited electronically into your checking account.

Compared to the other two RIGs, this solution produces the lowest amount of retirement income, so you'd use this solution only if it generates enough retirement income to help you cover your living expenses. I acknowledge that many people may not be in the position to use this solution, since they'll need to squeeze as much income as possible from their retirement savings. So here are some reasons you'd use this solution:

- if flexibility and access to your savings are very important,
- if you want to leave a legacy to your children or charities, or
- if the investment income is sufficient to cover your living expenses, which means you've managed to accumulate a substantial amount of retirement savings.

Here are two more very specific circumstances where this solution might make sense:

1. If you're working part time or with a reduced income, perhaps in your 60s or early 70s, you could supplement your employment income with your investment earnings. Then when you retire full time, you can switch to another RIG that provides a higher retirement income.

2. If you don't buy long-term care insurance and don't have any other substantial financial resources to pay for long-term care, such as home equity, you may want to consider using this RIG. In this case, if you don't tap the principal of your retirement savings, that money can act as a reserve if you eventually need to pay for expensive long-term care. However, you don't want to rely too much on your retirement savings for this reserve; long-term care can easily cost $50,000 per year or more. At that rate, it won't take too long to wipe out your retirement savings, unless, of course, you start your retirement with a boatload of money.

Choosing this solution will require periodic attention over your lifetime to make sure your investments continue to meet your financial goals in retirement.

Retirement income scorecard

Figure 7.1 shows the retirement income scorecard as of July 2012 for the five solutions presented in this chapter. This scorecard is for a married couple who are both retiring at age 65 with $100,000 in retirement savings. Whenever annuities are used, I assumed a 100% joint and survivor annuity was elected.

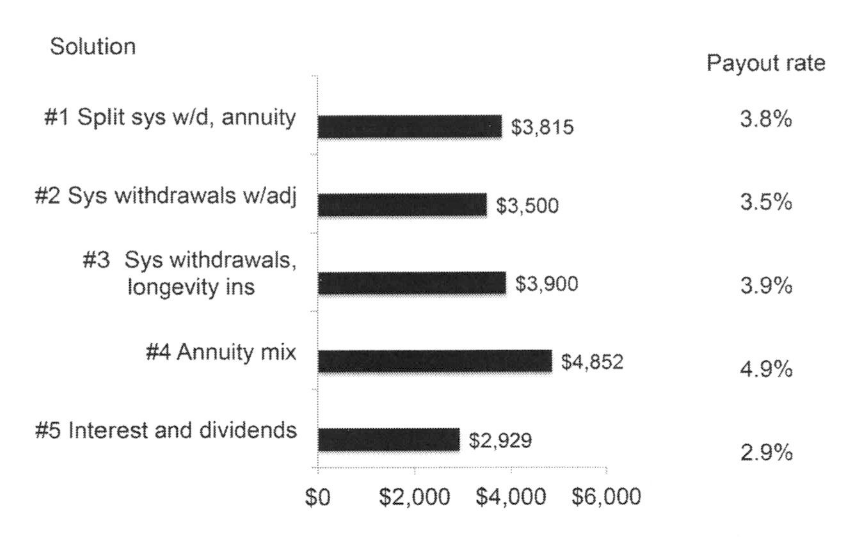

FIGURE 7.1 RETIREMENT INCOME SCORECARD: FIVE FAVORITE RETIREMENT SOLUTIONS

To prepare this chart, I made the following assumptions:

- ***Solution #1 (split between systematic withdrawals and annuity).*** I assumed a 50/50 split between an inflation-adjusted annuity and systematic withdrawals with an initial withdrawal rate of 4%. Compared to Solution #2, the presence of the inflation-adjusted annuity can justify a higher withdrawal rate on the portion of your savings that uses systematic withdrawals.

- ***Solution #2 (systematic withdrawals).*** I assumed an initial withdrawal rate of 3.5%. This rate would need to be revisited in future years as your investment experience unfolds during your retirement.

- ***Solution #3 (systematic withdrawals with longevity insurance).*** For this solution, I assumed you'd set aside 15% of your savings for a longevity annuity that starts at age 85, and that the initial payout rate would be 3.9% of your account balance.

- ***Solution #4 (immediate annuities).*** I assumed you'd devote one-third of your savings to an immediate fixed annuity, one-third to an immediate variable annuity, and one-third to the Vanguard Wellington fund to generate investment income.

- ***Solution #5 (interest and dividends).*** I assumed you'd invest in the Vanguard Wellington fund that's invested approximately 65% in stocks with the remainder in bonds and cash.

As you can see, Figure 7.1 shows a wide range of results for initial annual paychecks – from $2,929 to $4,852. This demonstrates what I've noted previously: The initial retirement income amount you generate can vary widely, depending on the particular RIG or combination of RIGs that you select. Each retirement income solution has its pros and cons, and each offers varying levels of protection against the risks of longevity and inflation. Because there's no single solution that works best in all circumstances, you'll have to choose the solution you think will work best for *you.*

The five solutions I've offered here are intended to help you think through the issues and decide which retirement paycheck solution best suits your circumstances. You don't have to choose any one of these solutions – you might have good reasons for deviating from these options. I believe you'll do best in your retirement years by making an informed decision after considering and analyzing a handful of viable choices. And you won't regret the time you spend thinking through the issues, when your retirement paycheck keeps chugging along in your 80s and 90s.

CHAPTER 8

How to Decide Which Solution Works for You

In Chapter 1, I introduced the ***Money for* LIFE™** five-step system that can help you choose the best retirement income solution for you. This chapter addresses Step 4 of this process: selecting the retirement income generator (RIG) – or combination of RIGs – that works best for you.

You may be able to select your retirement income solution just by reading the first seven chapters. If that's the case, you can skip this chapter and the next. If you need more help thinking through the issues, however, these next two chapters provide a systematic way to analyze and choose a retirement income solution that fits your goals and life circumstances.

The RIG – or combination of RIGs – that's most appropriate for you will depend on how much retirement income you need, how you want to balance the **LIFE** goals I described in Chapter 2, and your particular life circumstances. There's no silver bullet that works for everybody, and there's no magic formula you can use to make the decision for you.

But I can offer some help with your decision. This chapter helps you prioritize the **LIFE** goals that fit your circumstances, and suggests RIGs that best meet each of the **LIFE** goals. It also summarizes the rankings from previous chapters, comparing how the various RIGs meet each of the **LIFE** goals. Chapter 9 provides additional help with deciding which RIG meets your goals with a basic "win/regret" analysis.

Once you've narrowed down your choices to a few RIGs or combination of RIGs, you can estimate how much of a retirement paycheck you might generate from each method, and this chapter helps you with this task. This step can be a "moment of truth" for you, in that it's entirely possible the resulting retirement paycheck you calculate won't be enough to meet your estimated living expenses. In this case, you'll need to make some adjustments in critical assumptions, such as when you can retire or your estimated living expenses, and then repeat the process. You may also need to adjust your priorities for the **LIFE** goals.

Plan retirement like Mr. Spock,
not Homer Simpson!

I'll also discuss the considerations for determining how important each of the **LIFE** goals may be for you, and I'll suggest RIGs that best meet each goal. You may find it helpful to rank how important each of the following **LIFE** goals is for you, using a scale from 1 to 3, with 1 being of low importance and 3 being of high importance. You can use Table 8.1 to record your rankings:

Table 8.1 Your ranking of the LIFE goals

LIFE goal	Your ranking
Longevity protection	
Inflation protection	
Flexibility and Financial legacy	
Exposure to market risk	

These are all very personal issues to consider; your answers might be different from your co-workers, friends, and relatives.

One last note before we begin: When rating the RIGs, I've distinguished between two possible ways to implement systematic withdrawals:

1. Using a cautious withdrawal strategy, which involves making periodic adjustments as described in Chapter 7, and a low initial annual withdrawal rate – 3% or 3½% for people who are retiring in their mid-60s.

2. Using an optimistic withdrawal strategy, with few mid-course adjustments and using an initial annual withdrawal rate of 4% or higher for people who are retiring in their mid-60s. See Chapters 4 and 14 for more information on the initial withdrawal rate for the systematic withdrawal method.

LIFE goal #1: Longevity protection

When thinking about longevity protection, you'll give this goal a low rating if you have other sources of guaranteed lifetime retirement income that cover most, if not all, of your basic living expenses, such as Social Security or an employer-sponsored pension plan. You might also give it a low rating if you (and your spouse or partner, if applicable) are in poor health with a low life expectancy. On the other hand, you'll give it a higher score if your RIGs will need to cover a significant amount of your living expenses and if you have average or above-average life expectancy.

One way to think about the importance of this goal is to imagine how you'd feel if you exhausted your retirement savings during your retirement. Will you have a backup plan or other resources you can rely on, or will you be in deep trouble?

Now that you've ranked this goal, take a look at Table 8.2 that shows which methods might be best for you.

TABLE 8.2 RIGS THAT ARE APPROPRIATE FOR LONGEVITY PROTECTION

Rating	Appropriate RIG
1. Not important at all	Systematic withdrawals with an optimistic withdrawal strategy
2. Moderately important	Systematic withdrawals with a cautious withdrawal strategy
3. Very important	Investment income or immediate fixed, variable, or inflation-adjusted annuity, or a GLWB product

LIFE goal #2: Inflation protection

You will give the goal of inflation protection a low rating if you have other, significant sources of guaranteed retirement income that are indexed for inflation, such as Social Security or an inflation-adjusted pension. You'll also give it a low score if you've taken steps to manage your living expenses by doing such things as paying off your home mortgage, taking care of your health, buying adequate medical insurance, driving your cars into the ground rather than replacing them every few years, consciously reducing your utility or other monthly bills, and so on. You might also give it a low rating if you think your living expenses might decline in your later years due to reduced travel and recreational expenses. Don't rely too much on this last assumption, however, due to the possibility of increased expenses for medical and long-term care.

Conversely, you'll give this goal a higher score if your RIGs will need to cover a significant amount of your living expenses and if you haven't taken steps to contain increases in your living expenses.

As with the first **LIFE** goal, try to imagine how you would feel if your buying power were significantly eroded in the future due to inflation. Would you have other financial resources that you can tap? Or would you be able to reduce your living expenses substantially if the buying power of your retirement paycheck were eroded? Thinking about these issues will help you give this goal the most appropriate rating. Table 8.3 shows which RIGs might be best for you.

TABLE 8.3 RIGS THAT ARE APPROPRIATE FOR INFLATION PROTECTION

Rating	Appropriate RIG
1. Not important at all	Immediate fixed annuity
2. Moderately important	Investment income, immediate variable annuity, systematic withdrawals with an optimistic withdrawal strategy, or a GLWB product
3. Very important	Immediate inflation-adjusted annuity or systematic withdrawals with a cautious withdrawal strategy

LIFE goal #3: Flexibility and the potential for a Financial legacy

Now it's time to consider the third **LIFE** goal: flexibility and the potential to leave a financial legacy. You'll give this goal a low score if you don't have a big need to access your savings and have set aside a reserve for emergencies or other large expenditures. You'll also score this goal low if leaving a legacy to your children or charities isn't important to you. For example, you may have other assets that you can leave as a legacy, such as your home, jewelry, art, cars, and so on. On the other hand, you'll rate this goal higher if flexibility and access to capital are important to you and if you want to leave a legacy to your children or charities from your retirement savings.

Once again, imagine how you'd feel if you weren't able to leave a legacy to your children or charities. Is it more important to generate as much retirement income as you can at the expense of leaving a legacy? Or can you accept a reduced retirement income so that you're able to leave a legacy?

You also need to consider how important it is to you to be able to access your money whenever you want. But if you can access it – and spend it – it won't be there to generate retirement income for you. After rating this **LIFE** goal, take a look at Table 8.4, which shows the RIGs that might best fit your circumstances:

Table 8.4 RIGS that are appropriate for flexibility and financial legacy

Rating	Appropriate RIG
1. Not important at all	Immediate fixed, variable, or inflation-adjusted annuity
2. Moderately important	Systematic withdrawals with an optimistic withdrawal strategy or a GLWB product
3. Very important	Investment income or systematic withdrawals with a cautious withdrawal strategy

LIFE goal #4: Exposure to market risk is minimized

You will give the goal of exposure to minimal market risk a low rating if you have significant sources of lifetime retirement income that won't decrease during market downturns, such as Social Security or an employer-sponsored pension. You'll also give this one a low score if there's a large margin between your total retirement income and your estimated living expenses; if that's the case, you could probably tolerate a decrease in your retirement income if there's a market downturn.

If, on the other hand, you can't tolerate a drop in income and you're living "close to the edge," then you'll give this one a higher score. Something else to think about: How have you reacted during previous market declines? Did you lose sleep, or panic and sell your assets? Try to imagine how you'd feel in the future when the market declines, as it inevitably will. If you'd react negatively, give this goal a higher score.

After you've assigned a rating to this one, take a look at Table 8.5 that shows which RIG or RIGs might work best for you.

TABLE 8.5 RIGS THAT ARE APPROPRIATE FOR MINIMAL MARKET RISK

Rating	Appropriate RIG
1. Not important at all	Systematic withdrawals with an optimistic withdrawal strategy
2. Moderately important	Investment income, immediate variable annuity, or systematic withdrawals with a cautious withdrawal strategy
3. Very important	Immediate fixed or inflation-adjusted annuity, or a GLWB product

Once you've scored all the **LIFE** goals for yourself, compare your rankings to the summaries that follow to see how each of the RIGs rank with respect to the various **LIFE** goals. This will help you determine which RIG, or combination of RIGs, will work best for your circumstances and goals.

Goal	Investment income	Systematic Withdrawals Cautious	Systematic Withdrawals Optimistic
Amount of initial income	○	○	◑
Longevity protection	●	◑	○
Inflation protection	◑	●	◑
Flexibility and Financial legacy	●	●	◑
Exposure is minimized	◑	◑	○

● = high or strong
◑ = medium or maybe
○ = low or none

FIGURE 8.1 LIFE GOAL RANKINGS FOR INVESTMENT INCOME AND SYSTEMATIC WITHDRAWALS

Goal	Immediate fixed annuity	Immediate inflation-adjusted annuity	Immediate variable annuity
Amount of initial income	●	○	●
Longevity protection	●	●	●
Inflation protection	○	●	◐
Flexibility and Financial legacy	○	○	○
Exposure is minimized	●	●	○

● = high or strong
◐ = medium or maybe
○ = low or none

FIGURE 8.2 LIFE GOAL RANKINGS FOR IMMEDIATE ANNUITIES

Goal	GLWB/ GMWB	Financial Engines Income +	UBS Lifetime Income
Amount of initial income	◐	○	◐
Longevity protection	●	◐	●
Inflation protection	◐	◐	◐
Flexibility and Financial legacy	◐	●	◐
Exposure is minimized	●	◐	◐

● = high or strong
◐ = medium or maybe
○ = low or none

FIGURE 8.3 LIFE GOAL RANKINGS FOR HYBRID SOLUTIONS

Other ways to help you decide

There are sophisticated online systems available that can analyze your situation and make suggestions as to how to decide between the various RIGs (although they don't use this acronym). One example is MetLife's Retirement Income Selector, which asks nine questions about how you feel about certain financial goals in retirement. This survey takes just a few minutes to complete and bases its suggestions on your emotions – how you *feel* about certain retirement goals. It doesn't use numbers, and it isn't a calculator that estimates your retirement income. Because this system won't take very long to complete and offers helpful insights about the RIGs that might work well for you, I'd encourage you to test it out.

Another online system you might want to try is Fidelity Investments' Retirement Income Planner, which is a sophisticated online retirement calculator and planner. It asks a number of questions about your financial resources and helps you estimate your essential and discretionary retirement living expenses. It will also project your retirement income, along with the likelihood that you'll meet specified goals, and will make suggestions for dividing your retirement assets between systematic withdrawals and annuities. This survey takes about an hour, possibly more, to complete, but I'd recommend trying this system if you're also using it to calculate the budgeting estimates and projections of your retirement income.

Estimate your retirement paycheck

By now you've selected one or more preliminary retirement income solutions that you want to investigate further. The next step is to estimate the potential amount of your retirement paycheck using the solution or solutions you chose. Here's how you can do that:

- If you've chosen RIG #1 (investment income), you should be able to estimate the amount of annual income you'll receive from the dividend and interest yields of your specific investments. If you plan to use mutual funds, the fund sponsor should be able to show you the actual dividend payments during the past 12 months. If you haven't yet selected your investments, then you can estimate your annual retirement income by assuming an annual income of 2% of your retirement savings if you're primarily invested in stocks or 3% if you're invested in a balance of stocks and bonds.

- If you're thinking about using RIG #2 (systematic withdrawals), then determine your annual withdrawal rate and apply it to the total amount of your retirement savings to see how much money you'll be able to draw out annually.

- If you've chosen RIG #3 (immediate annuities), then you can use an online annuity bidding service to estimate your retirement income, based on the type of annuity you'll be buying, your age and sex, and the age and sex of your spouse or partner.

- If you've chosen a guaranteed lifetime withdrawal product (GLWB), you can apply the withdrawal percentage to your income base to estimate your retirement paycheck.

- If you're using a combination of RIGs, then apply the above steps to each part of your savings you're planning to allocate to each type of RIG to estimate your annual income.

The moment of truth

Now comes the "moment of truth." It's time to compare your estimated retirement paycheck to the amount of income you figured you would need in Step 3 of the five-step process I introduced in Chapter 1. You're in good shape if your estimated retirement paycheck, along with your other sources of retirement income, is big enough to meet your spending needs. If your estimated retirement paycheck falls short of your spending needs, however, you'll need to make compromises on one or more of the following items:

- your **LIFE** goals,

- the amount of retirement income you need,

- when you can retire, or

- whether you'll need to work a little in your retirement years.

If you have fallen short, you will need to make some changes to your plans and go through the tasks in this chapter until you're satisfied with the results.

And that's it! If one type of RIG emerges from these steps as the clear winner for your circumstances and lifestyle, you're done. But don't worry if two or more RIGs are still neck and neck at the finish line – that's entirely possible. This is actually a good outcome because it indicates that you might want to consider a combination of RIGs, a solution that offers the additional advantage of diversifying your retirement income, the next topic I'd like to touch on.

Diversifying your retirement income

You're most likely familiar with the idea of investment diversification – the "don't put all your eggs in one basket" theory of investing. An important refinement of this theory involves diversifying your retirement income. Since it's next to impossible for any of us to accurately predict when high inflation or a recession will occur, this strategy can protect your retirement income no matter what happens in the economy. To put this strategy into practice, you'll want to have different sources of retirement income that can withstand various types of economic challenges.

Table 8.6 summarizes why this is an important goal by rating how different sources of retirement income have fared in various economic climates.

TABLE 8.6 DIVERSIFY YOUR INVESTMENTS *AND* RETIREMENT PAYCHECK

	Social Security	Pension/ annuity	Stocks	Bonds	Cash**	Real estate	Hard assets***
"Normal" times*	Good	Good	BEST	Good	*Poor*	Good	*Poor*
Recession/ deflation	BEST	BEST	*Poor*	BEST	Good	*Poor*	*Poor*
High inflation	Good	*Poor*	*MIXED*	*Poor*	Good	*MIXED*	BEST

* Low inflation, steady economic growth
** T-bills, money market funds, FDIC-insured savings accounts
*** Gold, silver, commodities, collectibles, etc.

Note that the only source of income that does well in all three economic scenarios is Social Security benefits. Every other source of income does well in some economic climates but poorly in others. This is one reason why maximizing your Social Security income is a good strategy.

It's nearly impossible for most of us to accurately predict when the economic climates shown in this chart will occur. Also, given how long you'll be retired, there's a good chance you'll experience all three types of economic environments during your lifetime. That's why it's a good idea to diversify your sources of retirement income and choose more than one type of RIG.

Let me offer an example that illustrates what I mean. The first retirement income solution I suggested in Chapter 7 uses an immediate annuity to cover your essential living expenses and systematic withdrawals to cover your discretionary living expenses. The annuity provides a paycheck that's guaranteed to last the rest of your life, and the systematic withdrawals method offers flexibility and access to a portion of your retirement savings. Using both RIGs will help you realize the advantages of each while mitigating the disadvantages of both.

Don't give up!

I expect that you might need to repeat my ***Money for* LIFE™** five-step system a few times before you settle on a retirement paycheck solution that works best for you. But I think that's well worth your time and attention because this process will help you reexamine some very important life decisions. You may need to make some tradeoffs or compromises. But that's OK – remember that you're planning your retirement security for the rest of your life.

If you are working with a financial planner, you'll want to show your planner how you ranked each of the **LIFE** goals. Your planner may also be able to help you complete the tasks in this chapter, particularly by estimating the amount of your retirement paycheck under the solutions you're considering. Your planner can also help you select the appropriate products or institutions to implement your retirement income solution.

It's also critical to realize that your goals and circumstances can change as you age, and there can be good reasons to change your retirement income solution(s) during your retirement years. For instance, you might like to use RIG #1 (investment income) in your 60s and 70s, particularly when you might be working part time to supplement your retirement income. Then, when you get into your 80s, you may desire low maintenance, predictability, and protection against longevity risk, which would call for investing more of your retirement savings in RIG #3 (an immediate annuity).

Remember that deciding on a retirement income solution is part art, part science. Gather as much information as you can, and prepare the necessary analyses. Also pay attention to your gut feelings – they're sometimes the best judge of what's best for you. Talk things over with your spouse or partner, as well as close relatives and friends whom you trust and have your best interests at heart. It always helps to share with others when making important life decisions.

If you invest the time now to learn how to generate a retirement income that best meets your retirement needs, you'll have the peace of mind later to focus on what's really important – the rest of your life!

CHAPTER 9

Win/Regret Analysis

If you're still having trouble deciding which of the three RIGs and their variations would work for you, try using a way that doesn't involve numbers. Instead, think about the consequences of your decision with a simple, yet systematic, win/regret analysis. For each method of generating retirement income, this analysis (shown below in several charts) reveals the circumstances when you "win" or when you "regret" your decision and what it is you will win or regret.

TABLE 9.1 WIN/REGRET SUMMARY

Win/regret circumstance	RIG #1 Investment income	RIG #2 Systematic withdrawals	RIG #3 Immediate annuities
You live longer than your projected life expectancy	Win	Regret	Win
You die before your projected life expectancy	Regret	Win	Regret
Your investment returns are better than expected during your retirement	Win	Win	Regret
Your investment returns are worse than expected during your retirement	Regret	Regret	Win

Looking over this list, think about how you feel about the odds of each win/regret circumstance. For example, do you think you'll die before or after your projected life expectancy? Or achieve better-than-expected or worse-than-expected investment returns during your retirement?

Now let's compare the consequences of your RIG choices for each type of RIG:

Table 9.2 Win/regret consequences for investment income

Win/regret circumstance	**RIG #1 Investment income**
You live longer than your projected life expectancy	*Win* – You enjoy a retirement paycheck that lasts for as long as you live.
You die before your projected life expectancy	*Regret* – You could have spent more money during your retirement years.
Your investment returns are better than expected during your retirement	*Win* – You can increase your spending or leave a legacy.
Your investment returns are worse than expected during your retirement	*Regret* – You may need to reduce your spending, but you're not broke.

Table 9.3 Win/regret consequences for systematic withdrawals

Win/regret circumstance	**RIG #2 Systematic withdrawals**
You live longer than your projected life expectancy	*Regret* – You might go broke and need to reduce your spending or move in with your kids.
You die before your projected life expectancy	*Win* – Money's left over when you die, and your heirs and charities thank you.
Your investment returns are better than expected during your retirement	*Win* – You can increase your spending or leave a legacy.
Your investment returns are worse than expected during your retirement	*Regret* – You might go broke and need to reduce your spending or move in with your kids.

TABLE 9.4 WIN/REGRET CONSEQUENCES FOR IMMEDIATE ANNUITIES

Win/regret circumstance	RIG #3 Immediate annuities
You live longer than your projected life expectancy	*Win* – You enjoy a retirement paycheck that lasts for as long as you live.
You die before your projected life expectancy	*Regret* – You've left money with the insurance company to pay other policyholders (but you're dead, so how much do you really care?).
Your investment returns are better than expected during your retirement	*Regret* – You could have done better had you used RIG #1 or #2 instead.
Your investment returns are worse than expected during your retirement	*Win* – You enjoy a retirement paycheck that keeps coming in no matter what happens in the economy.

Looking at the second set of tables, how do you feel about the consequences of each circumstance? For me, the consequences of regret with systematic withdrawals – going broke in my later years and needing to move in with my kids – are pretty high. The level of this regret is higher than the potential gain I would get from winning with systematic withdrawals by leaving a legacy. And I'm nervous about having to rely on good investment returns – which I have little control over – in order to win. But with an immediate annuity, it's the other way around. If I live a long time, I enjoy a long life and steady income, rather than worrying about living so long that I'd need to move in with my kids.

If you look at this second set of tables closely, you'll see that the circumstances and consequences of winning vs. regretting complement each other for the various RIGs. This is another good reason to diversify your retirement paycheck and use a hybrid approach, as described in Chapter 6. By doing so, you're more likely to get the best of both worlds when it comes to your long-term outcomes.

I admit the above analysis is somewhat simplistic, but I wanted to make it easy to understand. Digging deeper, you'll see that one way to mitigate the "regret" circumstances is by modifying the way you implement each RIG.

For example:

- With systematic withdrawals, choosing an initial cautious withdrawal rate with adjustments and a backup plan can mitigate the regret circumstances, making this option more of a win for you.

- Deciding to use a GLWB product can mitigate some of the regret circumstances for annuities, also turning your regret into more of a win.

A win/regret analysis is just one way to think about how best to generate a retirement paycheck from your savings without getting too wrapped up in the numbers. Don't ignore the numbers completely, however, as the amount of retirement income you'll be able to generate will depend significantly on the method you choose, and you'll want to work the numbers to determine how much money you can expect to generate.

For example, in 2012, a given amount of retirement savings will generate roughly the same amount of retirement income whether you use an immediate fixed annuity or an immediate variable annuity. Similarly, a given amount of retirement savings will generate approximately the same amount of retirement income using an immediate inflation-adjusted annuity or systematic withdrawals with a cautious withdrawal strategy, but the amount you'll need to invest is higher compared to immediate fixed or immediate variable annuities.

Think carefully about how much income you will really need, as well as the advantages and disadvantages of each method. Take the time to consider how you feel about the odds of winning and losing with each method and how much you care about the consequences. Talk it over with your spouse or partner, or close friends who care about you. This method offers another way to win – and you won't regret the time you spend doing your research when you reach your 80s or 90s knowing you made the best choice for you.

CHAPTER 10

What's Your Retirement Number?

Now that we've reviewed the process for determining just which lifetime retirement paycheck generator meets your goals and circumstances, there's just one question left: How much retirement savings do you really need in order to leave the workforce for good?

If you're seriously considering retiring soon, this is an important task that you should not do casually. Nor should you accept a general, fixed number that you might have read is the goal for most people. Instead, you should calculate the retirement savings *you* need, taking into account your own circumstances and preferences. There's been a lot of press about what your ideal "retirement number" should be, so let's see how you can best estimate that number.

You'll need to do the first four steps of the ***Money for*** **LIFE™** system that I described in Chapter 1 before you get to this fifth and final step: calculating your retirement number. To help you easily understand each of the steps and see how they all go together, below I've described all five steps and included an example – a married couple, both the same age, who are considering retiring at age 65.

Step 1: Estimate your projected life expectancy.

As I described in Chapter 1, it's important to get an estimate of how long you might live so you'll know how long your money needs to last. If you're married or in a committed relationship, you'll also want to estimate your spouse or partner's life expectancy. If you haven't yet done this first step, go back to Chapter 1 to see how to complete it.

For our example, let's assume the married couple used the websites shown in Chapter 1 and find out that the husband can be expected to live to age 89 and the wife might live to age 92. Because they might live a long time, it's important that their retirement paycheck be guaranteed to last for their lifetimes.

Step 2: Take inventory of your retirement resources.

You should start the inventory of your resources by adding up the values of all your retirement savings, so you can compare this amount to the result of Step 5 in this exercise, to see when you can afford to retire.

It's also critical to determine how much annual lifetime retirement income you can expect to get from sources other than your retirement savings, such as Social Security and a work-related pension, if you're lucky enough to participate in such a plan. Again, hopefully you've already estimated these amounts as part of your homework from Chapter 1. If you haven't, go back and do that now.

For our example, let's assume the couple's annual Social Security income will be $24,000 when you consider both of their incomes – that's close to the average for people this age, according to the Social Security Administration. Let's also assume neither the husband nor the wife will be receiving a retirement paycheck from a traditional, employer-sponsored pension plan.

Step 3: Figure out how much money you'll *really* need.

After you retire, your annual living expenses can be dramatically different from your current annual living expenses because your circumstances may change dramatically. Hopefully you've already estimated your living expenses as part of your "prepping and sanding" in Chapter 1. If you haven't done that yet, go back to Chapter 1 and work through the steps to figure out this number.

Then add up all your sources of retirement income from Step 2, and subtract this amount from the estimate of your retirement expenses. The remainder is the amount you'll need to generate from your retirement savings – your retirement paycheck.

For the purpose of our example, let's assume the married couple estimated their annual retirement living expenses to be $50,000, including income taxes. If we subtract the $24,000 Social Security income the couple will be receiving from their retirement budget of $50,000, you'll see they'll need to generate a $26,000 annual retirement paycheck from their retirement savings in order to cover their annual expenses.

Step 4: Decide which method or methods you will use to generate a retirement paycheck.

As you've seen in previous chapters, the various methods of generating a retirement paycheck produce different amounts of retirement income. So it's only natural that your decision regarding which method to use to generate a retirement paycheck will dictate exactly how much retirement savings you will need to have on hand to generate that paycheck.

Your next step is to choose a method of generating a retirement paycheck, or a combination of methods, based on what works best for your circumstances, and then determine the payout rate. The payout rates for various retirement income generators (RIGs) were shown in the retirement income scorecards in Chapters 3, 4, 5, and 7. You may need to work with a financial planner to estimate the payout rate for your specific retirement paycheck solution.

For our example, let's assume the couple decides to split their retirement savings 50/50 between an inflation-adjusted annuity and the systematic withdrawal method with a 4% withdrawal rate. The Social Security income and the annuity income are both guaranteed to last the rest of their lives, while the income from the systematic withdrawal will hopefully also last for life, although it's not guaranteed.

In this case, our couple's combined payout rate would be 3.8%, as shown in the retirement income scorecard in Chapter 7 for the first retirement income solution described in that chapter.

Step 5: Estimate your retirement number.

Finally, you're ready to calculate your retirement number! To do this, you'll want to invert your payout rate; for those of you who forgot your high school algebra, just divide the number "1" by your payout rate. In this example, that would be 1 divided by .038, which equals 26.32.

Then multiply this factor by the results you got in Step 3 – the amount of annual retirement income you need to generate from your retirement savings. In this example, you would multiply $26,000 by 26.32 for a result of $684,320. That's the retirement number in this example – the amount of retirement savings this couple needs to have on hand in order to retire and no longer work.

Keep in mind, you'll also want to have a reserve for emergencies and other large expenditures, such as deductibles for medical expenses, a new car, or large household items. This reserve should be separate and in addition to the savings you'll use to generate your retirement paycheck. You'll want to pad the retirement number you came up with by $20,000 to $50,000 to cover this reserve. In our example, adding in an emergency reserve could bring this couple's total retirement number to $725,000.

The resulting "retirement number" in this example is well above the average retirement savings of many Americans who are currently in their mid-60s. If this couple's savings are below this amount, they'll need to consider some ways to make their situation work, such as working longer or reducing their expected *discretionary* living expenses.

While calculating your retirement number may seem like a lot of effort, it's a much better method than just guessing, which is what many people do. And most people guess too low, with the inevitable, unfortunate result that they'll run out of money before they pass away. You'll be glad you made the effort to estimate how much retirement savings you really need when you reach your 80s and 90s and your retirement paycheck keeps rolling in.

Making your "golden" years a reality

How can you thrive and really enjoy your retirement? Take the time *now* to do the math to see if your retirement paycheck will cover your anticipated living expenses for the rest of your life by using the following "magic formula" for retirement security:

I > E, or

Income > Expenses

The homework you have done as part of Chapters 1 and 8 will help you estimate both sides of this formula to determine if your income will be higher than – or at least equal to – your expenses.

But what happens if you've done your homework and you just can't make the numbers work for retirement at your current age? When *can* you retire?

You can make a big difference just by delaying your retirement for a few years – say, from two to five years. So it's a good exercise to project your retirement paycheck at different ages – say, at 62, 65, and 70 – to help you determine your retirement finish line.

While you're still working for those few extra years, your Social Security income will increase because you've delayed the start of benefits and, most likely, so will your pension, if you participate in a defined benefit plan. The Social Security website can show you how your expected income will increase if you delay benefit commencement. If you participate in a defined benefit plan, you can also project what your retirement income would be in a few years through an online calculation system, if there's one available for your plan, or by calling your plan administrator.

You'll also want to project the increase in your retirement paycheck from your retirement savings if you delay retirement. Here's a step-by-step approach for doing that:

Step 1: Project your account balance.

I'd use a simplified, conservative approach to determine this amount. Just take the total amount of your current retirement savings from all sources – 401(k), IRA, and so on. Add any additional contributions you expect to make between now and your future retirement date. I wouldn't bother adding any investment earnings, given the current low interest rates and stock market volatility. If your account balances do grow with investment returns, it's only gravy.

Step 2: Estimate your retirement paycheck.

For the retirement income generator (RIG) or combination of RIGs that you've chosen, apply the payout rates to your projected account balances from Step 1 above.

If you use RIG #1 (investment income) or RIG #2 (systematic withdrawals), just assume the current payout rates will apply in the future. This should be appropriate if you're only delaying retirement by up to three years. If you're delaying retirement by four years or more, you may be able to increase your withdrawal rate for systematic withdrawals by half a percent (0.50%) to reflect the fact that you'll be receiving payments for a shorter period.

If you've decided to use RIG #3 (immediate annuities), your retirement paycheck will definitely increase each year you delay your retirement. You can get an estimate of what the increase will be by using the online annuity shopping services mentioned in Chapter 5. Note, however, that annuity purchase rates may increase between now and when you plan to retire, so you may want to build in a cushion for that possibility.

If you decide you need to keep working for a few more years, you've got lots of company – many people are putting off retirement, either because they want to stay busy and connected or because they need the income. But you don't have to stick with the status quo. Instead, look for ways to make work more enjoyable, maybe by reducing your hours or responsibilities, and by starting to participate in some of the activities you hoped to enjoy during your retirement. And don't be too bitter about delaying your retirement – I've found fascinating research that suggests people who work in their retirement years are healthier and may even live longer.

It's likely you'll need to repeat the analyses in this chapter for a few different retirement ages until you can make the numbers work for you. You may even want to work with a financial planner to help you with these estimates and to decide when you can afford to retire. You won't regret the time and effort you make to do the job right.

CHAPTER 11

Working With Financial Advisors

Generating reliable retirement income for the rest of your life no matter how long you live is an ambitious undertaking that takes time and skill. It's entirely understandable that you might want to seek the advice of a professional financial advisor to help you with this task. After all, you can't afford to make mistakes, and you'll need to make every dollar count. One goal of this book is to help you have an informed conversation with your financial advisor.

If you are considering working with a financial advisor, you should be aware that there are advisors who could be a danger to your retirement security: advisors who don't have the necessary skills or expertise when it comes to generating a lifetime retirement income, or who are more interested in making money for themselves than for you.

Of course, there are also advisors who are trustworthy and have taken time to be trained on the specialized skills needed to generate a lifetime retirement income. Your job is to find a trusted financial advisor who will take your goals and circumstances into account and then help you choose the best methods for generating a lifelong retirement income. This chapter helps you with this important task.

Credentials and experience to look for

Let's start by distinguishing between investment advice and retirement planning. An investment advisor might be good at helping you decide what your asset allocation should be and selecting specific securities or mutual funds – all the advice you really needed while you were growing your nest egg.

But using your retirement savings to generate retirement income is more complex, and you'll need a retirement planner who is experienced with helping people decide which retirement income generator (RIG), or combination of RIGS, will work best for you.

To this end, you should look for an advisor with credentials that require substantial training and experience with financial planning. Examples include Certified Financial Planners (CFP), Chartered Financial Analysts (CFA), Certified Public Accountant - Personal Financial Specialist (CPA-PFS), and Chartered Financial Consultants (ChFC). These credentials all show evidence of training on a broad variety of financial planning topics.

But be aware that these credentials focus on asset investment and accumulation without much of an emphasis on generating lifetime retirement income. As a result, I recommend that you ask potential advisors if they have supplemented their training or expertise with specialized training on the various methods of generating retirement income. Three examples of this are the Certified Retirement Counselor (CRC) designation from the International Foundation for Retirement Education, the Retirement Management Analyst (RMA) designation from the Retirement Income Industry Association (RIIA), and the Retirement Income Certified Professional (RICP) from American College. These designations are fairly new, so it may not be easy to find advisors with these credentials. At the very least, ask the advisor how they have been trained on the various methods of generating a retirement paycheck and whether they're able to explain the pros and cons of each method.

A funny story

Here's an amusing story that illustrates how easy it can be to get an impressive-looking credential. CBS MoneyWatch blogger and financial planner Allan Roth has a fancy plaque hanging on his office wall from Consumers' Research Council of America – it's an award for "America's Top Financial Planners." The council's address is on Pennsylvania Avenue in Washington, DC. After seeing this plaque, wouldn't you feel pretty confident working with Allan?

Look a little more closely, however, and you'll see the name on the plaque is Max Tailwager – the name of Allan's dachshund puppy. According to Allan, all he had to do to get this plaque was to provide the company with his credit card number and Max's name. The moral of the story? Don't be fooled by the fancy plaques on the wall! Be sure to ask any advisor you're considering working with for the specifics regarding the training and experience they needed to earn their credentials.

A sad state of affairs

Would you be surprised to hear that retail financial advisors often recommend the portfolio that makes the most money for *them*, not their customers, even if their recommendations result in less money for their clients or make their client's current situation worse? That's the damning conclusion of a working paper published by the National Bureau of Economic Research reporting on an audit conducted by the Consumer Financial Protection Bureau (CFPB) regarding the quality of financial advice.

The CFPB put together a clever undercover operation in which trained auditors visited numerous retail financial advisors whom the average citizen can access via their bank, independent brokerage, or independent advisory firm. These advisors are usually paid based on the commissions and fees they generate from transactions and not on the assets under management. The audit was carried out in the Boston area in 2008.

The goal of the audit was to determine if the financial advisors would attempt to correct investing mistakes that individuals might be making or if they would exploit those mistakes and move their customers toward funds that generated high fees. An important goal of the audit was to estimate the extent to which advisors gave "good advice," defined as moving investors towards low-cost, diversified index funds, a strategy suggested by many investment textbooks and one often recommended by experienced financial consultants, including my fellow CBS MoneyWatch bloggers Allan Roth and Larry Swedroe.

The auditors presented the advisors with one of four scenarios:

1. The auditor expressed a desire to chase returns – that is, to invest in an industry sector fund that had performed well during the previous year.

2. The auditor held 30% of his or her portfolio in the company stock of their imaginary employer.

3. The auditor held a diversified, low-fee portfolio consisting of index funds and bonds – in effect, an efficient portfolio often suggested by textbook theory.

4. The auditor held all of his or her investments in CDs and simply expressed a willingness to increase risk for higher returns.

Particularly troubling was what happened if the auditor presented the diversified, low-cost portfolio (scenario #3): In 85% of the cases, the advisor suggested changing the investment strategy. In just 2.4% of these visits did the financial advisor support the low-cost portfolio. Since having a low-cost portfolio has been repeatedly demonstrated to be the most efficient way to invest, the advisors' suggestions would most likely result in lower savings for their customers. In effect, the advisors were willing to make a change that would make their clients worse off.

This is the sad state of affairs facing many middle-class investors who are seeking help to generate a reliable retirement income. But there are actions you can take to protect yourself, so read on.

How is your advisor paid?

It is very important to make sure your advisor has no incentive other than to act in your best interests when advising how to generate retirement income. This often includes help choosing between annuities and investing. So one important thing to find out is how your advisor is paid. Having a trained professional whose compensation is aligned with your best interests can increase the odds that your retirement nest egg will turn out sunny side up – not scrambled.

My least favorite way to pay for retirement planning advice involves paying someone a commission or sales charge on investments or insurance. With this method, advisors may be tempted to direct you to the investments or insurance policies that pay them the highest commissions. They may also be tempted to churn your account – which means to buy and sell your investments frequently to generate commissions on every sale and purchase. Because commissions can range from 2% to 10% or more, on a $100,000 transaction, you'd be paying $2,000 to $10,000 on each transaction!

Fee-based planners are a better choice because in theory, they shouldn't have a stake in your investing decisions. However, even here you need to be careful. The most common fee-based arrangement is to charge you a percentage of your assets that are under the advisor's management; 1% is a common charge. And while 1% sounds small, it can really add up over the years. For example, suppose you have $400,000 in retirement savings. With this amount under the advisor's management, you'd be charged $4,000 per year, year after year. After 10 years, you'll have paid your advisor $40,000 in fees – money you could have spent on yourself!

In addition, an advisor who charges an annual fee may not be too thrilled to recommend an immediate annuity – which might be a good choice for you – since those assets won't be subject to the advisor's charges.

My favorite way to pay for retirement planning advice is to find someone whom you pay by the hour or on a flat fee basis. Typical hourly rates range from $150 to $300, while a typical project fee could be $1,000, $2,000, or more. Although that flat fee may sound high, it often works out to be less than 1% of your assets under management. And it's comparable to the amount you might pay an attorney for estate planning or other legal matters. In many cases, an hourly-based advisor will give you a fee quote for a specific project, so you'll know exactly how much you'll spend in total.

A good hourly planner should also set you up with a plan to generate retirement income that doesn't need constant attention. So instead of paying a fee every year, as you would with a percent of assets under management, you can pay for a periodic checkup or a review if an important event, such as the death of a spouse or a market meltdown, requires attention to your investments.

Even with hourly planners, however, there are no guarantees, so watch out for planners who put together complex plans that would require them to spend many hours each month monitoring your investments. All planners will have their biases, based on their background and training, but paying your advisor by the hour has the best chance of minimizing these biases. Still, you'll have to ask the right questions before committing to any advisor.

Two networks of fee-based financial planners I'd suggest you investigate are Garrett Planning Network and the Alliance of Cambridge Advisors. Both of these planning organizations have national networks of advisors who meet specified standards for training and experience. These two suggestions are just starting points for your investigation, since there can be many qualified advisors near you.

Also, I should point out that many financial advisors who charge a percent of assets under management would also be willing to charge a flat fee or by the hour if you only ask them, so don't reject these type of advisors outright without investigating their fees further. If you can't find a planner who charges by the hour, then the percent of assets under management is the next best approach. Be sure to have them explain the pros and cons of the different methods of generating retirement income.

Questions to ask your financial advisor

Before you select the financial advisor you'd like to work with, here's a checklist of questions you should ask every potential financial advisor you're considering. These questions will help you more thoroughly evaluate your options.

1. *How do you charge for your services?* As noted previously, you'll want to avoid planners who earn money through commissions and instead seek planners who charge a flat rate or at least just a percentage of assets under management.

2. *What experience and training do you have that's relevant to my situation?* Find out how long the advisor has been in practice and the companies with whom they've practiced. Also ask if he or she has any professional certifications, licenses, or designations, such as the ones I mentioned earlier. Don't forget to inquire about special training, experience, and expertise at generating retirement income, which is different from asset accumulation and investing.

3. *What is your approach to generating retirement income?* Find out if they'll work with you to decide which RIG – or combination of RIGs – will work best for you. Avoid planners who express any biases toward one method without first learning about your goals.

4. *Can you provide me with three or four references?* Request contact information for two or three current clients whom they advised on generating retirement income, as well as one professional reference, such as an accountant or estate attorney.

Then ask *yourself* two important questions:

1. *Do I like this person?* You'll work better together if you mesh well with this person and enjoy spending time with them. You may be interacting with this person for a long time, so it helps to choose someone with a personality you like. You'll also need to feel you can trust this person, since you'll be revealing all your financial "secrets" so the advisor is fully informed about your situation.

2. *Do I understand this person?* Hopefully he or she won't use jargon and will tell you just enough for you to understand the issues. It's not necessary for the advisor to tell you everything they know about a subject just to impress you; often all that does is confuse matters.

If you're married or in a committed relationship, find out whether your spouse or partner likes and understands this person, too. After all, you're hiring someone who will be very important to your financial security for the rest of your life. If you have any reservations, move on. There are plenty of qualified advisors out there who are able and willing to help you out and whom you're sure to bond with.

Don't feel shy about asking these questions or insulting the advisor. A good planner welcomes the opportunity to be of service. Ditch any planner who makes you feel uncomfortable in any way.

Four danger signs

When hiring a financial advisor, remember that you're buying something from them: their services. Having been on the receiving end of enough sales pitches from financial advisors and having heard numerous horror stories about unscrupulous or uninformed advisors from participants in my retirement planning workshops, I'd like to offer some advice about what to watch out for.

Here are four statements coming from a financial advisor that should raise red flags with you:

1. *When you retire, roll your 401(k) account out of your plan at work. I can deliver better returns.*

Most likely, this is the wrong move to make if you work for a large company – say, one with 1,000 employees or more. In this case, it's very likely that your employer's HR or finance department has shopped around for high-performing funds with below-average investment expenses; they may have even been able to negotiate special deals on investment fees because of the number of people participating in the plan.

On the other hand, this advice could work out right if you work for a smaller employer whose 401(k) plan has retail mutual funds with high fees. So my advice is this: Do your homework. Compare the level of investment management fees of the funds in your employer's 401(k) plan to the fees the investment advisor is planning to charge you. If your advisor uses mutual funds, you should also compare the historical investment performance of these funds and the ones in your 401(k) plan.

2. *If you're offered a lump sum from your pension plan at work, take it. I can deliver good investment returns that will generate a higher retirement income than a monthly pension check.*

This type of statement reflects a poor understanding of the value of a lifetime guarantee offered by the typical employer-sponsored pension plan. Most people in average or excellent health are better off taking the lifetime annuity from their pension plan at work because they will live long enough to realize a higher lifetime payout. (If you want more details on this topic, the "Resources" section of my website www.restoflife.com includes an article that contains a checklist on whether to take an annuity or lump sum from a defined benefit pension plan.)

3. *Start taking your Social Security benefits as soon as possible, and invest them with me, even if you don't need the income. I can help you realize investment returns that will generate more retirement income for you.*

Once again, this statement reflects a poor understanding of the value of the lifetime guarantee offered by Social Security benefits. The reality is, this strategy only produces higher retirement income if you take significant risks in the stock market or if you're unhealthy and are likely to die before your projected life expectancy.

4. *Invest with me, and your annual retirement income can be a lot higher than 4% of your retirement savings.*

As I have already noted in Chapter 4, the four percent rule should be a starting point for an informed discussion about the level of withdrawal that's appropriate given your circumstances. And even that long-standing four percent rule is being questioned these days, given our current low interest rates and the level of investment advisor fees.

The four percent rule is based on the assumption that over the long run, you will achieve returns similar to returns on stock and bond indices. Yet some advisors boast that their superior returns can generate higher retirement income for you. If you hear an advisor promising high returns, be very wary. It's likely that such an advisor has just talked you into taking a higher risk of outliving your savings and that they really can't deliver superior returns over the long run, after expenses, that support a higher withdrawal rate. Studies have repeatedly shown that very few active managers can beat passively managed index funds. If your advisor's recommendations produce returns lower than the indices, you've only increased your chances of outliving your savings.

It's much better to be cautious with your initial withdrawals and then increase them down the road only after an advisor's recommendations have actually delivered a solid investment performance for several years.

So why would advisors make the statements described above? If their charges are based on assets under management, which is common for fee-based planners, then they'll want a lot of your money to manage. This is one reason I recommend you purchase financial advice by the hour or for a specified project; this way, your advisor doesn't have a monetary incentive to tell you things that may help them get more of your money to manage.

The bottom line is, you need to find a competent advisor who's qualified to help you understand the pros and cons of the different ways you can generate a lifetime retirement income. You also want someone who listens to you and asks questions about your specific circumstances before making any recommendations. While it's not an impossible goal, it will require some time and effort on your part.

How can an advisor add value?

In addition to finding an advisor who charges fairly for his or her services and has your best interests at heart, it's also important to realize the ways that a financial advisor can realistically add value to your retirement planning. It makes sense for an advisor to help you with these decisions and tasks:

- how to generate a retirement paycheck,
- how to allocate your assets between stocks and bonds given your preference for taking risk,
- periodically rebalancing your investment portfolio to keep it in line with your asset allocation preferences,
- how to minimize your taxes,
- which investments have low costs and reasonable investment histories, and
- when to begin taking your Social Security benefits.

They might also help you with estate planning considerations.

On the other hand, studies have shown that most advisors will not be able to beat stock or bond market indices with their investment advice – in fact, they often produce lower returns over the long run. It's also not realistic to expect them to achieve superior returns through their ability to actively manage stocks, bonds, and mutual funds, or by "timing the market."

Two final thoughts about seeking help:

When you get to your 60s and beyond, you might consider getting help from professionals who are younger than you. Once you've found great people to work with, you don't want them to retire before you do!

If you're married or in a committed relationship, you should involve your spouse or partner with the selection of a financial advisor and the ongoing planning. You'll want their understanding and acceptance of the strategies you develop. And if you pass away first, they'll need to understand the strategies that you've developed with your financial planner.

All of this may sound like it will take a lot of time and effort. Don't let that deter you. The best way to achieve your goals is to go shopping – *don't be sold!* Spend the time necessary to find the type of person who best meets your needs; don't be sold by someone whom you happen to meet in a social situation or who's been recommended by a friend and talks a good story.

Put a lot of thought into choosing a financial advisor who will help you generate a reliable lifetime paycheck. After all, you're planning for your financial security for the rest of your life. The thoughts and stories in this chapter are not intended to scare you away from working with financial advisors; in fact, the right financial advisor can be essential to your retirement security. Doing your homework now to help you choose wisely will save you a lot of heartache in the future.

WRAP-UP

Let's wrap up Part One here. The following chapters are resource chapters for those of you who want more details on the specific RIGs.

You'll do best in your retirement years if you can rest assured you'll have a retirement paycheck for the rest of your life. So take the time to analyze the various methods of generating retirement income – learn about their pros and cons, and see how much income each RIG will generate for you. This may take many hours, but that's OK. You're planning for a retirement paycheck that needs to last a long time – 20 years or more – and putting in the effort now means you'll be able to rest easier later.

People like choices, and this is particularly important for your retirement security. Heed the words of my good friend Toni Brown, who is the head of defined contribution investment consulting for the human resources firm Mercer and the 2012 - 2013 president of the Defined Contribution Institutional Investment Association (DCIIA):

Imagine you hadn't tasted ice cream before and someone introduced you to vanilla ice cream. You might be quite happy for awhile. But what if a few years later you discovered chocolate and strawberry? Wouldn't you have wondered what you missed all those years? It's the same with choosing a retirement paycheck – you'll be best served if you understand all your options and make an informed choice.

You want to live with dignity and fulfillment in your retirement years. If you take the time to plan for a secure retirement paycheck, you can turn your attention to more important things, like spending time with family and friends, pursuing your interests, taking care of your health, and helping make the world a better place.

Best wishes for your retirement years!

PART TWO

THE DETAILS

In Part One, you learned about the different types of retirement income generators (RIGs), including how to analyze which solutions might be best for you, how to best shop for them, and how to work with financial professionals who can guide you through the process. Now it's time to learn more about taxes, investment strategies, safe withdrawal rates for systematic withdrawals, and insurance company products and guarantees. The chapters in Part Two can help you refine your strategies for investing and minimizing income taxes during your retirement.

I've constructed these chapters to be more like appendices that serve as resources to deepen your understanding of the topics we discussed in Part One. They may not be as "pretty" as the earlier chapters – you'll find no illustrations and not as many charts that emphasize the main points, as in Part One. The information they provide, however, will help you more fully understand the critical issues you need to be aware of in order to generate a lifelong retirement paycheck from your savings.

If you're working with a financial advisor and/or tax professional who's handling such issues as taxation, investing, safe withdrawal rates, and insurance company guarantees, you may be able to skip these chapters. But it can be in your best interests, even if you're not dealing directly with these issues, to be aware of them so that you're as informed as possible while you're working with an advisor. After all, it's your money we're talking about here, and the buck stops with you. So I'd suggest you take some time to review Part Two to familiarize yourself with these issues. You won't regret investing the time now to help yourself down the road.

CHAPTER 12

Taxes Matter!

Analyzing and choosing the best retirement income generator (RIG) is essential to creating a stream of retirement income that will last as long as you live no matter what happens in the economy. But so is maximizing the amount of money you get to keep after paying federal and state income taxes on that income. That's why you need to learn just how your retirement paycheck will be taxed, which depends significantly on the RIGs you use to generate your retirement paycheck.

In addition to understanding how your income will be taxed, you'll also want to learn how you can avoid falling into a few tax traps that can result in unpleasant penalties. Although understanding the rules isn't rocket science, you do need to pay attention to some of the details to avoid tax issues later. It might also be a good idea to check with a tax accountant while you're setting up your RIGs to make sure you aren't missing an opportunity to decrease your income taxes or to prevent yourself from getting caught in a tax trap.

The tax rules that will apply to your income will depend on where and how your retirement savings are invested, as well as the specific RIG, or combination of RIGs, you choose to use to generate your retirement paycheck. This chapter outlines some of the rules and offers some strategies to consider.

But before we dive into the various tax rules and strategies that apply to your retirement paycheck, I think it's a good idea for you to have a basic understanding of the federal income tax structure.

What's your marginal tax rate?

Federal income taxes are progressive, meaning that the different levels of taxable income are taxed at increasingly higher rates. You can understand this by looking at Table 12.1, which shows ordinary income tax rates for individuals and married couples for 2012.

TABLE 12.1 ORDINARY INCOME TAX RATES FOR 2012

Tax rate	Taxable income single	Taxable income married filing jointly
10%	$0 - $8,700	$0 - $17,400
15%	$8,701 - $35,350	$17,401 - $70,700
25%	$35,351 - $85,650	$70,701 - $142,700
28%	$85,651 - $178,650	$142,701 - $217,450
33%	$178,651 - $388,350	$217,451 - $388,350
35%	Over $388,350	Over $388,350

It's important to understand that:

- the above tax rates apply to your taxable income, which is your total income after you've subtracted exemptions and deductions,
- your taxable income may include a portion of your Social Security income, as discussed later in this chapter, and
- the tax brackets are different for married filing separately or head of household.

For example, suppose you're married filing jointly, and your taxable income is $75,000 after applying deductions and exemptions. Here's how your federal income tax would be calculated:

- The first $17,400 of your taxable income would be taxed at 10%, which results in a tax amount of $1,740.
- Your taxable income between $17,400 and $70,700 would be taxed at 15%, which results in a tax amount of $7,995 (15% of $70,700 minus the $17,400 that was taxed at 10%).

- Your taxable income between $70,700 and $75,000 would be taxed at 25%, which results in a tax amount of $1,075 (25% of $75,000 minus the $70,700 that was already taxed).

In this example, if you add up the amounts for each layer of your taxable income, the total federal income tax you owe would be $10,810.

The tax that applies to your highest layer of income is called your "marginal tax rate." Think of it as the rate that would apply to one more dollar of income above your current income. Many readers will probably fall in the 15% or 25% brackets during their retirement. Count yourself lucky if you're in a higher tax bracket – although you'll pay higher taxes, it also means you're making good money! You should take the time to estimate your marginal tax rate to see if it's worth the effort to implement strategies during your retirement that will minimize your income taxes.

In addition to federal income taxes, most states (but not all) impose their own income taxes on retirement income generated from savings. The tax rate schedules for these states are usually progressive, like federal income tax rates, but the tax brackets are different and the tax rates are lower. You'll want to estimate your combined federal and state marginal tax rate for the purpose of minimizing your income taxes.

A maximum federal income tax rate of 15% applies in certain situations for investments held outside of any tax-advantaged account such as IRAs or 401(k) accounts. This 15% rate applies to gains on the sale of individual securities or mutual funds that are held for more than one year; these are known as "long-term capital gains." The 15% rate also applies to dividends paid to investors from most stock investments, whether that's from individual securities or stocks held in mutual funds. The 15% rate applies to these investments even if the marginal tax rate on your other income is 25% or higher.

It's important to note that as this book goes to press, our political leaders are hotly debating the tax rates that apply to ordinary income, long-term capital gains, and qualified dividends for 2013 and beyond. The rates could go up or down in future years, depending on the political party that has the most influence. It's likely that any changes won't be finalized until well after the 2012 elections; if the debate continues well into 2013, any new rates may be postponed until 2014. Be sure to stay tuned!

Now let's turn to the tax rules that will apply to your various sources of retirement income.

Tax rules for traditional IRA and 401(k) accounts

The tax rules are pretty simple for the part of your retirement savings that you invest in a deductible IRA, 401(k), 403(b) plan for nonprofit employers, 457(b) plan for government employers, or other tax-advantaged account. The money you invested in these accounts was pre-tax income, which means you didn't pay any federal income taxes on these funds. Because of that, when you withdraw a retirement paycheck from these accounts, the money will be subject to ordinary federal income taxes. Most (but not all) states will also apply income taxes to the withdrawals you make from a tax-advantaged account. This is the case whether you're using RIG #1 (investment income) or RIG #2 (systematic withdrawals) to generate a retirement paycheck. It's also the case regardless of the type of investment you use, whether that's stocks, bonds, cash, or some other type of investment.

There's one exception, and that's for amounts held in the stock of your employer; these are subject to the rules regarding net unrealized appreciation (NUA). These rules are complex and beyond the scope of this book, so if you have substantial amounts in your 401(k) plan that are invested in your company's stock, you'd be best served consulting a tax accountant who's familiar with the NUA rules.

If you decide to use RIG #3 (immediate annuity) to generate a retirement paycheck, you'll want to tell the insurance company you work with that the purchase amount of the annuity is coming from a deductible IRA, 401(k), 403(b), or 457(b) account, and make sure they get you into a tax-qualified annuity. This way, you won't be taxed immediately on the full value of the annuity purchase. Instead, the monthly income you receive each calendar year will be subject to ordinary federal income taxes for that year. This tax situation will apply for the rest of your life and the life of any beneficiary whom you designate on the annuity. Again, most (but not all) states will also tax your income from an annuity.

Required minimum distributions: a trap for the unwary

For some tax-advantaged retirement accounts – deductible IRAs, 401(k)s, 403(b)s, or 457(b)s – Uncle Sam wants to make sure that you eventually pay income taxes on the money you have in these accounts. So our good uncle applies required minimum distribution (RMD) rules that start when you turn age 70½. While you'd have to be a tax accountant to understand all the intricacies of the RMD rules, the basic concepts are fairly easy to understand, so I'll outline them in order for you to see how they might affect your retirement paycheck. Before we dig into the details, however, note that the word "distribution" is IRS jargon for "payment," so choose the word that makes you feel more at ease when reading my explanations below.

Let's begin with the first rule you need to know: In the year you turn age 70½, by December 31 of that year, you'll be required to withdraw minimum amounts and include these amounts in your taxable income for that year. If you withdraw amounts that add up to less than the minimum, the amount of the shortfall will be subject to a 50% penalty tax! You'll want to make absolutely sure you withdraw at least the minimum amounts necessary to comply with the RMD rules.

Normally you'll need to make these withdrawals by December 31 of each year. In the first year the RMD rules apply, however, the IRS allows you to delay taking the minimum withdrawal as late as April 1 of the year following the year you reach age 70½. For every year thereafter, however, you'll need to withdraw the RMD amounts during each calendar year. If you elect to delay making the withdrawals as late as April 1 in the first year the rules apply to you, you'll need to make two withdrawals during that year: by April 1 for the withdrawal that applies to the previous year and by December 31 for the withdrawal that's required for the current year.

Using age 70½ as the threshold for the RMD rules sometimes creates confusion about when the rules apply. Think of it this way: If your birthday is on or between January 1 and June 30, your 70½ year is the year you also reach age 70. If your birthday is on or between July 1 and December 31, your 70½ year is the year after you reach age 70.

The RMD rules don't apply to the following investments:

- Roth IRAs while the owner is alive,
- employer-based retirement plans, such as 401(k) accounts, if you're still working for the company that sponsors the plan, i.e., if you haven't yet retired from that employer. If you own 5% or more of that business, however, the RMD rules apply at age 70½ even if you're still working at that business, and
- investments held outside of any tax-advantaged account.

The RMD you'll have to pay is based on the value of your accounts as of December 31 of the previous year. The IRS requires that you divide this value by the "distribution period" for each age to determine the RMD you owe. To help you out, I've done the math for you. Table 12.2 shows the distribution period and the minimum payout rate for each age (these figures apply to the majority of situations).

TABLE 12.2 PAYOUT RATES RESULTING FROM RMD RULES

Age	Distribution period in years	Minimum payout rate
70	27.4	3.65%
71	26.5	3.77%
72	25.6	3.91%
73	24.7	4.05%
74	23.8	4.20%
75	22.9	4.37%
76	22.0	4.55%
77	21.2	4.72%
78	20.3	4.93%
79	19.5	5.13%
80	18.7	5.35%
81	17.9	5.59%
82	17.1	5.85%
83	16.3	6.13%
84	15.5	6.45%
85	14.8	6.76%
86	14.1	7.09%
87	13.4	7.46%
88	12.7	7.87%
89	12.0	8.33%
90	11.4	8.77%

A few essentials to note:

- Although I stopped the table at age 90 for brevity's sake, the IRS table continues beyond age 90.

- For Table 12.2, if you're the account-holder, use your age on your birthday during the calendar year.
- If you're married and your spouse is more than 10 years younger than you, a different table with payout rates that are lower than the above rates applies in your situation.
- A separate table also applies to beneficiaries after the account holder has died.

If you have more than one IRA, you must calculate the amount of the RMD separately for each IRA, although you're allowed to withdraw the total amount you owe from just one of your IRAs. Similarly, if you have more than one 403(b) account, you must calculate the RMD separately for each 403(b) account, but you can take the total amount you owe from just one of your 403(b) accounts. If you have more than one 401(k) or 457(b) accounts, you must calculate the RMD separately for each account *and* you must also withdraw the RMD you owe on each account from each specific account.

If you're using RIG #1 (investment income) or RIG #2 (systematic withdrawals), your withdrawals might fall short of the required minimum distribution. For example, if you've decided to withdraw 4% from your account each year using systematic withdrawals, by age 73, you'll fall short of the RMD you're required to make. In this case, you would need to withdraw more, but you don't need to *spend* the withdrawals – you just have to withdraw the money and include it in your taxable income. Then you can invest the money you had to withdraw in an after-tax savings account.

If you use RIG #3 (immediate annuities), you automatically comply with the RMD rules. That's because your paychecks are spread out over your expected lifetime, and the IRS assumes you have legitimately retired and aren't using IRA or 401(k) accounts to play games with federal taxes. This can be yet another reason to consider an immediate annuity in your later years: In addition to all the other decisions you'll need to make to manage RIGs #1 and #2, you'll have to continue to worry about complying with the RMD rules. But you won't have these worries with an annuity.

If your retirement paycheck comes from a guaranteed lifetime withdrawal benefit (GLWB) product, you'll want to check with your insurance company on what you need to do to comply with the RMD rules. Most insurance companies will provide guidance on how their GLWB products comply with the RMD rules.

To help you more fully understand how the RMD rules work, here's an easy example. Suppose your birthday is March 1, 1943, and you turn age 70 on March 1, 2013. In this case, 2013 is the year you need to start complying with the RMD rules. Your RMD amounts will be based on your account values as of December 31, 2012, the year before your 70th birthday. Let's suppose this account value is $100,000. To determine your RMD for 2013, divide $100,000 by 27.4 years, for a result of $3,650. This amount needs to be withdrawn by December 31 of 2013 and included in your 2013 taxable income.

Just for your first year of complying with the RMD rules, however, you can elect to delay compliance into 2014. If you take advantage of this special rule, you'll have two taxable withdrawals in 2014: one for the RMD for 2013 that you're delaying into 2014, and one for the regular RMD you'll need to take for 2014.

Because a complete description of the RMD rules is beyond the scope of this book, I encourage you to consult either a tax accountant; your IRA, 401(k), 403(b), or 457(b) plan administrator; or an online source to learn more. Your IRA or 401(k) institution may be able to calculate the RMD for you, but the ultimate responsibility for complying with these rules lies with you (in other words, you're still on the hook if your IRA or 401(k) institution makes a mistake). Be sure to check the calculations yourself so you know you're paying exactly what you owe and don't get hit with a penalty later.

Early distribution penalties: another trap for the unwary

With deductible IRA, 401(k), and 403(b) accounts, the RMD rules discourage you from waiting too long before making withdrawals. There are also rules – and penalties – in place that discourage you from making withdrawals too early; after all, these accounts are supposed to be for your retirement, so the federal government wants you to think twice before withdrawing the funds for anything else.

The general rule regarding early withdrawals is fairly straightforward: With deductible IRAs and employer-sponsored 401(k) and 403(b) plans, any amount that you withdraw before attaining age 59½ is subject to a 10% penalty tax. This penalty tax is in addition to any ordinary income taxes that you'll pay on the amount of your withdrawal.

There's an important exception that applies to employer-sponsored retirement plans such as 401(k) and 403(b) plans: The 10% penalty does not apply to withdrawals you make after attaining age 55, provided that the withdrawal is due to your termination of service from your employer and that you separated from service after attaining age 55. In other words, if you retire early from your employer and you're at least 55 years old, you won't be subject to the early withdrawal penalty.

Note that this exception only applies to amounts you withdraw from the tax-advantaged plan of the company that you retired from after age 55. If you have other 401(k) accounts from previous employers where you terminated employment before age 55, you'll need to wait until age 59½ before making a withdrawal in order to avoid an early withdrawal penalty.

There are a few more important exceptions to the early distribution rules for deductible IRA, 401(k), and 403(b) accounts. These situations occur if:

- you buy an immediate annuity with payments that are expected to be made over your lifetime,
- you don't buy an annuity but instead make withdrawals that are intended to be spread out over your lifetime,
- the payment is to an alternative payee under a Qualified Domestic Relations Order (QDRO) in the event of a divorce,
- withdrawals are needed to pay for qualified medical expenses that exceed 7.5% of your adjusted gross income, or
- withdrawals are due to the death or permanent disability of the employee or account-holder.

If you're considering *any* withdrawal before attaining age 59½, I would strongly suggest you consult a tax accountant or financial planner to make sure you aren't subject to the early distribution penalty.

Tax rules for Roth IRAs and Roth 401(k), 403(b), and 457(b) accounts

Here the rules are pretty simple: Because your contributions to a Roth IRA or Roth 401(k), 403(b), or 457(b) account were included in your taxable income for the year you made these contributions, you don't owe any additional federal income taxes on them. So during your retirement, any withdrawals you make from these accounts, whether that money comes from your contributions or your investment earnings, are tax free. To be eligible for this tax treatment, however, your withdrawal needs to take place at least five years after you established the Roth IRA or Roth 401(k), 403(b), or 457(b) account.

Now let's address the RMD rules. Although Roth IRAs aren't subject to the RMD rules mentioned earlier, Roth 401(k), 403(b), and 457(b) accounts are. If you want to escape the RMD for your investments in an employer-sponsored Roth account, you can roll this account to a Roth IRA.

Withdrawals of your original contributions to Roth IRAs or Roth 401(k), 403(b), and 457(b) accounts also aren't subject to the early distribution penalties noted above. If you withdraw your investment earnings before age 59½, however, the amount of that withdrawal would be subject to the early distribution penalty. The exceptions noted above for deductible IRAs also apply for Roth IRAs; there are also a few additional exceptions for the first-time purchase of a home or to pay for qualified educational expenses.

Again, if you're considering making *any* withdrawal before age 59½, I'd advise you to check with a tax accountant to be sure you aren't subject to the early distribution penalty.

Tax rules for after-tax savings

If you have savings that are held outside of a tax-advantaged account such as an IRA or 401(k), here's a brief summary of the tax rules that apply:

- You won't be charged any income tax if you withdraw your original principal.
- Any interest income you earn from bonds, CDs, and savings accounts will be taxed at ordinary income tax rates, though there are a few exceptions. For instance, interest from municipal bonds (the bonds of state and local governments) are usually exempt from federal income taxes and are often exempt from state income taxes as well.
- Long-term capital gains and dividends from qualified stocks are taxed by the federal government at a 15% income tax rate.
- If you buy an immediate annuity with savings you've held outside of a tax-advantaged account, then part of each monthly payment is deemed to be a return of your principal and isn't subject to income taxes. But the remaining part of your monthly payment is deemed to be interest and is subject to ordinary income tax rates. Your insurance company will compute the breakdown between return of principal and interest so you know exactly how much of your annuity will be taxed.

Tax rules for Social Security benefits

It's important to understand the particular rules that apply to Social Security benefits, because the rules can have an impact on how much tax you'll pay on your retirement paycheck from your savings. Depending on the total amount of your income in retirement, part or all of your Social Security income will be excluded from your taxable income, which means you'll have more to spend.

Here's a summary of the rules that apply to Social Security benefits. First, take one-half of the amount of your Social Security benefits and add it to all your other income, including any amounts payable from your RIGs that are included in your taxable income as well as any tax-exempt interest income on municipal bonds. If you're married filing jointly, you'll want to be sure to include the Social Security income of both you and your spouse. Then compare this amount to the two thresholds shown in Table 12.3 that are defined by the IRS rules.

TABLE 12.3 THRESHOLDS FOR TAXING SOCIAL SECURITY INCOME

Filing status	Base threshold	Additional threshold
Single or head of household	$25,000	$34,000
Married filing jointly	$32,000	$44,000

The amount of your Social Security income that's eligible to be taxed depends on how the total you computed compares to these thresholds:

- If the total falls below the base threshold, none of your Social Security income will be included in your taxable income.
- If the total falls between the two thresholds, then half of the amount of your Social Security income that exceeds the base threshold will be included in your taxable income.
- If the total is more than the amount listed in the "additional threshold" category and you're single, then the amount of your Social Security income that's included in your annual taxable income will be $4,500 plus 85% of the amount of your Social Security income that's over the additional threshold.
- If the total is more than the amount listed in the "additional threshold" category and you're married filing jointly, then the amount of your Social Security income that's included in your taxable income will be $6,000 plus 85% of the amount of your Social Security income that's over the additional threshold.

It's important to note that the above thresholds are not indexed for inflation, whereas most other tax brackets and thresholds are. What that means is that, as time goes on, more and more people will have their Social Security income subject to income taxes.

Regardless of your total income, at least 15% of your Social Security income will be exempt from federal income taxes. This special tax treatment is one reason why maximizing your Social Security income is a good strategy.

Now let's turn our attention to some possible strategies you can use to minimize your income taxes.

Tax strategy #1: Liberate the maximum amount of income that will be taxed at the lowest rate.

If you're using either investment income or systematic withdrawals to generate your retirement paycheck, you have some control over how much you can withdraw each year. In this case, you can minimize your income taxes if your taxable income from all sources fluctuates substantially from year to year. For example, suppose one year your taxable income is well below the threshold for the 25% federal income tax rate but that you expect your taxable income will be well above this threshold in a subsequent year. This can happen if you expect to receive additional taxable income from other sources in future years; one example of this situation is if you're delaying your Social Security benefits and you expect a large portion to be included in your taxable income when you do start receiving benefits. Or you might have unusually large tax deductions, such as for medical expenses, in the current year that you don't expect to continue in future years.

If this happens to you, it might make sense to withdraw enough money from your deductible IRA or 401(k) accounts so your annual taxable income lands right under the threshold of the 25% tax bracket, even if you don't need the full amount of your withdrawals to meet your living expenses. This action "liberates" some of your retirement savings to be taxed at the 15% rate instead of the 25% rate. You can then invest any money you don't need for current living expenses in an after-tax account; this saves the money to meet living expenses in a future year when your tax bracket is well above the threshold for the 25% tax rate and when you'll be trying to minimize your taxable withdrawals. If you have Roth accounts, you could also make withdrawals in future years to meet your living expenses; these withdrawals aren't subject to income taxes. You may need to work with a tax accountant to make this strategy work; an expert can help you estimate the maximum withdrawal amounts that would keep you below the 25% threshold.

This technique can also work in reverse. For example, if your current marginal tax rate is 25% or higher but you expect it to be lower in future years, you can make withdrawals from after-tax investments or Roth accounts in the current year instead of from tax-advantaged accounts. This lowers the amount of income taxed in the current year. This only works if you expect your marginal tax rate to drop in future years, when you'd make withdrawals from your deductible IRAs or 401(k) accounts. But watch out for the RMD rules that may apply after you attain age 70½.

Tax strategy #2: Take advantage of the 15% tax rate on long-term capital gains and qualified dividends.

This strategy can work for you if your taxable income is well into the 25% marginal federal income tax bracket or higher and you have savings in tax-advantaged accounts – such as IRAs and 401(k)s – as well as savings outside these types of accounts. If this describes your situation, it pays to have your stock investments in after-tax accounts and your bond investments in tax-advantaged accounts.

By having your stock investments in after-tax accounts, you can take advantage of the special 15% income tax rate on long-term capital gains and qualified dividends. This rate won't apply to stock investments held in tax-advantaged accounts.

But don't let tax considerations trump your investment strategies. If you have most of your retirement savings in tax-advantaged accounts and you're invested in stocks because of their long-term growth potential, it may be OK to keep these accounts in stocks. In other words, consider how you want to allocate your assets between stocks and bonds for *all* your retirement savings, considering both after-tax and tax-advantaged accounts. Then, to the extent that's possible, use after-tax accounts for your stock investments.

Tax strategy #3: Use index funds to enjoy after-tax savings.

This tax strategy only applies to retirement savings held in mutual funds outside of tax-advantaged accounts, such as IRAs or 401(k)s. Here's the secret upside to this type of account: If you have money invested in a mutual fund and don't sell it for an entire calendar year, you still might receive a deemed distribution of taxable capital gains if your mutual fund has sold securities during the same year at a gain. These types of gains are usually zero or are minimal for index funds, since these funds don't do much selling of securities. When you consider that index funds usually outperform actively managed funds over the long run, you've got a powerful financial incentive to use index funds for your retirement savings instead of actively managed funds that buy and sell securities frequently.

Tax strategy #4: Use municipal bonds for more after-tax savings.

This strategy also only applies to any retirement savings held outside of tax-advantaged accounts, such as IRAs or 401(k)s. If your marginal federal tax rate is 25% or higher, you might consider using municipal bonds for the part of your investments that you usually invest in bonds. Unlike other bonds, interest on municipal bonds is exempt from federal income taxes and most state income taxes.

Tax strategy #5: Coordinate your withdrawals from tax-advantaged accounts with the start of your Social Security benefits.

As noted previously in this chapter, more of your Social Security benefits will be included in your taxable income as your total taxable income increases. Let's suppose you're delaying the start of Social Security benefits to increase your lifetime payout from Social Security. In this case, you may want to make withdrawals from your deductible IRA or 401(k) accounts before you start your Social Security benefits in order to reduce the amount of Social Security income that will later be included in your taxable income.

Here's one variation of this strategy to consider: Before you start receiving Social Security income, make withdrawals from your IRA or 401(k) accounts to pay off the mortgage on your house. This way, you'll reduce your ongoing living expenses and help reduce the amount of future Social Security payments that are subject to income taxes.

Tax strategy #6: Coordinate your withdrawals from tax-advantaged accounts to fall below Social Security thresholds.

If you plan ahead, you might be able to time withdrawals from deductible IRA or 401(k) accounts to minimize the amount of your Social Security income that's included in taxable income. This means managing your total income so that it falls below the additional threshold levels described in Table 12.3 – $34,000 if you're single, $44,000 if you're married.

But be careful if you're making large withdrawals from IRA or 401(k) accounts. If they're large enough, your withdrawals could increase the amount of your Social Security income that's subject to income taxes.

When you're setting up your RIGs, it might make sense to visit a tax accountant or financial planner. An expert can help you develop a course of action for your specific situation that minimizes federal and state income taxes, and avoids early distribution penalties before age 59½ or RMD penalties after age 70½.

Whew! If your head is spinning by now, take a deep breathe, but don't let all this information stop you from learning all you can about retirement taxes in order to find ways to minimize them. It's well worth your time to try to maximize the amount of retirement income you get to keep after paying federal and state income taxes.

CHAPTER 13

Managing Your Investment Risks

When it comes to your retirement paycheck, you'll be forced to make some essential choices involving investment risk. One of them is this: Are you willing to accept the possibility that your retirement paycheck might decrease due to poor investment performance in return for the chance to realize income increases if your retirement savings perform well? If you view this as an unacceptable gamble, your answer is probably "no." But if you see this as a calculated risk, your answer might just be "yes."

Your views on this question and other investment issues are important considerations when it comes to choosing the retirement income generators (RIGs) that will work best for you. Your investment choices will impact the amount of retirement income you'll receive throughout your retirement as well as the extent to which you're able to leave a legacy to your children or charities. As a result, you'll want to devote some time to seriously considering the investments that underlie your retirement paychecks.

When weighing your options, you can choose to insulate your retirement paycheck from market fluctuations, so there's no chance your income will decrease for reasons beyond your control. Or you can expose your retirement paycheck to the risk that it might decrease due to stock market declines or increases in interest rates in return for growth potential in your retirement paycheck if your investments perform well. A middle ground would be to accept some risk for the potential for growth but limit the potential for unacceptable decreases in your retirement paycheck.

In this chapter, we'll take a closer look at the investment considerations for the three primary RIGs described in Chapters 3, 4, and 5. But first, let's review some significant investment findings for balancing investment risk and return and the importance of investment management fees.

Balancing investment risk and return

As you research investment options for your retirement savings, you'll no doubt come across various expert opinions on retirement investing, including how best to allocate your retirement savings between stocks, bonds, and cash investments. You'll want to learn as much as you can about the potential risks and rewards of the different methods of investing and make decisions that you're comfortable with. For many readers, a good source on investing basics will be your savings plan at work or the websites of some of the large mutual fund providers, such as Fidelity Investments, Schwab, T. Rowe Price, or Vanguard.

In this chapter, I'll offer my opinions on the most appropriate investments for retirement savings. First, let's address the issue of asset allocation. I'd suggest you allocate your retirement savings between stocks, bonds, and cash investments as follows:

- Invest no less than one-third of your retirement savings in stocks and the balance in bonds and cash to give your savings and retirement paycheck the potential for growth, and

- Invest no more than two-thirds of your retirement savings in stocks and the balance in bonds and cash to protect yourself against stock market crashes.

So how would such a portfolio have fared during the 2008 - 2009 stock market crash? Many low-cost mutual funds with asset allocations falling in this range recovered all their losses by the fall of 2011, surpassing their highest values just before the crash. They took about three years to recoup their losses (provided that investors didn't make any withdrawals during this period). That's not bad for the worst investment period since the Great Depression!

One of the best ways to balance investment risk and return is to invest in low-cost, no-load mutual funds that are balanced between stocks, bonds, and cash investments, and possibly real estate investment trusts (REITs), another type of investment that offers the potential for appreciation. The mutual funds described in Chapter 3 suit this purpose well; you may want to look back to see which ones I suggest. You may also have low-cost index funds in your 401(k) plan at work, so check with your plan administrator to find out.

By the way, a no-load fund doesn't charge a commission against your investments; with a load fund, a one-time commission ranging from 2% to 6% is subtracted from your investment and paid to an agent, broker, or financial advisor.

The importance of investment management fees

Numerous financial experts have repeatedly demonstrated the importance of using low-cost (meaning low fee) index funds for the portion of your retirement savings that you'll invest in stocks. Over long periods of time, such funds have outperformed most actively managed portfolios with much higher fees. My advice is that you resist sales pitches for high-cost mutual funds that come with claims that they can beat the averages. If you give in and invest, you'll most likely be the loser – since these funds generally don't beat the averages – while the person who sold you these funds will be the winner, raking in high investment management fees from you year after year.

Allan Roth and Larry Swedroe, two financial experts and bloggers at CBS MoneyWatch, have repeatedly shown the value of low-cost index investing – check out their blogs if you want evidence for this conclusion. They've both shown that if you can achieve returns on your portfolio equal to the *average returns* – including dividends – on stock market indices, such as the S&P 500 or the Wilshire 5000, then you'll most likely beat the returns achieved by the *average investor.* This is due to the negative impact of high investment management fees on the balance of a portfolio and to the fact that most actively managed mutual funds underperform the index returns over long periods of time. Swedroe has even demonstrated that you can be an *above-average* investor by achieving *average* returns!

If you're wondering exactly what a "low cost" mutual fund is, I define it as a no-load fund with annual investment expenses below 0.50% – and the lower the better. You can find many index funds from Fidelity Investments, Schwab, and Vanguard with investment management expense ratios ranging from 0.10% to 0.30%. Many of you might also have funds with low fees in your 401(k) plan; new fee disclosures for 401(k) plans that go into effect during 2012 will enable you to better assess and compare the fund fees in your 401(k) plan.

Now let's turn to the investment considerations for the various types of RIGs.

Investment considerations for RIG #1: investment income

If you have a considerable retirement nest egg whose investment income can cover your living expenses, then using RIG #1 (investment income from interest and dividends) to generate your retirement paycheck is most likely a good choice for you. This drawdown method is also a good choice if leaving a legacy to your children or charities is important to you. With this method, your investment goals should be to generate an income stream with the potential for growth that won't decrease beyond tolerable levels due to market fluctuations, and that provides for modest growth in the principal for your legacy.

Using these guidelines, it would be a mistake to stretch for the highest-yielding stocks or bonds, since these investments often carry some risk that the dividend or interest payments can't be sustained. For you, investing in a broad-based group of stocks and bonds that include all types of companies is often the best choice.

Let's take a look to see how investing to withdraw just interest and dividends from a balanced portfolio might have fared during the 12-year period from 2000 through the end of 2011, which contained two stock market crashes. For the purposes of this example, let's assume you invested $200,000 on January 1, 2000, in Vanguard's Wellington Fund, which is invested 65% in stocks, with the remainder in bonds or cash investments.

Figure 13.1 shows that your annual retirement paycheck from interest and dividends would have been about $7,760 in 2000 and would have dropped to about $5,580 in 2003 due to the tech bubble bursting at the beginning of the century. Then your paycheck would have increased to about $7,830 by 2007, and dropped again to $6,820 by the end of 2011. As of December 31, 2011, your original $200,000 investment would have been worth $227,266, an increase of 13.6%. During those 12 years, you would have also received a total of about $53,000 in capital gains distributions, which you could have used to either smooth out your income stream or add to your invested account value at the end of 2011.

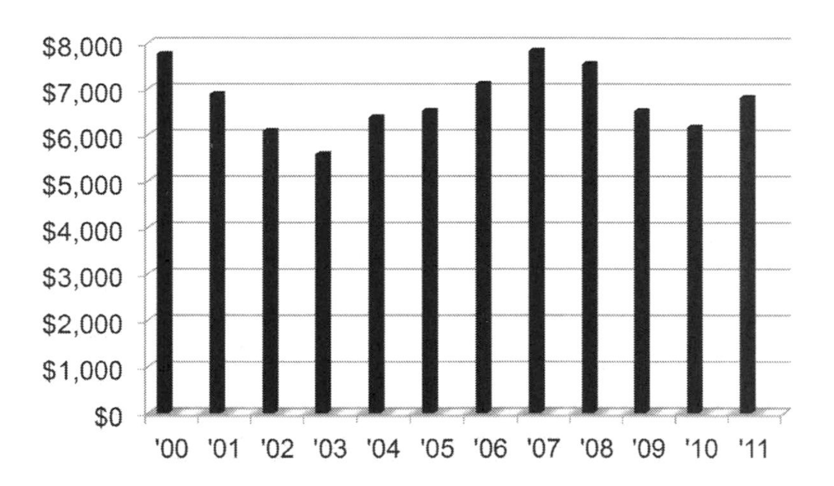

FIGURE 13.1 MODEST FLUCTUATIONS IN DIVIDEND INCOME STREAM

Now let's assume you had invested that $200,000 in a different fund –Vanguard's Wellesley Fund – with about 40% in stocks and the remainder in bonds or cash investments. Figure 13.2 shows that your annual retirement paycheck from interest and dividends would have been about $11,400 in 2000, would have dropped to about $9,030 in 2004, increased to about $10,640 by 2008, and then dropped again to $8,840 by the end of 2011. As of December 31, 2011, your original $200,000 investment would have been worth $246,559, an increase of 23.3%. During those 12 years, you would have also received a total of about $31,560 in capital gains distributions, which you could have used to either smooth out your income stream or add to your invested account value at the end of 2011.

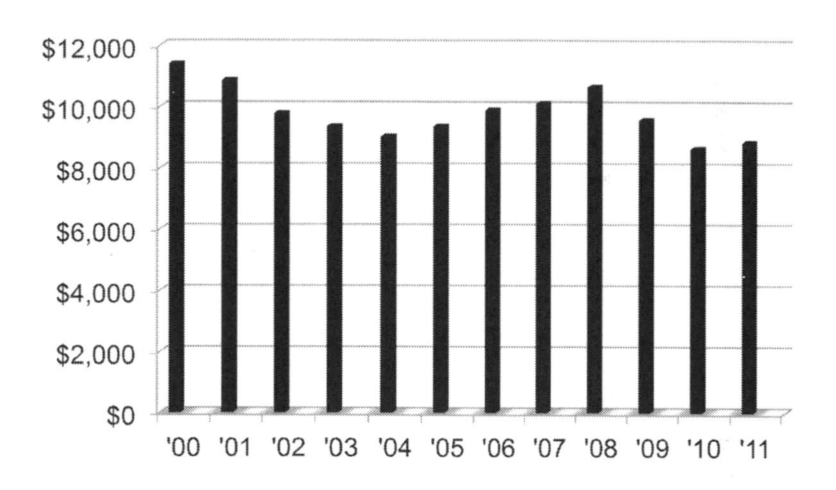

FIGURE 13.2 EVEN MORE MODEST FLUCTUATIONS IN DIVIDEND INCOME STREAM

When you compare the performance of these two funds, their underlying asset allocations explain the varying results these funds yielded. The Wellesley fund has a higher allocation to bonds than the Wellington fund does. This is the reason this fund earned investors a higher stream of income and provided reduced volatility in the stream of investment income over the course of the 12-year investment. And because bonds have appreciated due to a significant drop in interest rates since 2000, the Wellesley fund has appreciated more than the Wellington fund. This result isn't likely to be repeated in future years, however, due to the low interest rate environment in 2012.

I'd also like to point out that the Wellington and Wellesley funds are not index funds, but they do have investment management fees of less than 0.50%, and their asset allocation falls within the range suggested earlier in this chapter.

Now let's consider the investing results of these funds: If you had invested in either one of these funds and lived off the income stream, you would have survived one of the worst periods in investing history, with a relatively steady stream of income and your retirement savings intact. Many retirement investors fared a lot worse.

During tough times, your investing goal is to *survive* – it's unrealistic to expect significant growth in your retirement savings. The very simple investment and drawdown strategy described here would have enabled you to survive not one, but two stock market crashes. Your savings also would not have been wiped out, and you wouldn't have needed to make drastic changes in your lifestyle. And you would have kept your principal intact for the day when you might need to increase your retirement paycheck by drawing down your principal or buying a low-cost immediate annuity.

The pros and cons of rental income

I occasionally hear from people who advocate buying and managing rental properties as a retirement income source, comparing the rental income from rental properties to interest and dividends generated from stock and bond investments. Indeed, I know a few people who've made this option work for them. They've developed an income stream that's increased over time, and their property values had also been increasing until the most recent economic meltdown. Since they bought and held their rental properties for many years, they aren't currently underwater on the mortgages, and they have positive home equity in spite of the recent downturn.

If you have the time and skill to successfully manage real estate, this could be a possibility for you. Realize, however, that you need to consider whether you have the patience to assess potential tenants, the temperament to handle tenant relationships, and the skills to make the necessary home repairs when needed. Of course, you could pay a management company and/or handyman to carry out these tasks for you, but doing so would eat into your returns.

My wife and I became accidental landlords when her mother needed to move into an assisted living facility and she needed the rental income from what had been her primary residence to cover her living expenses. From this experience, I can tell you that being a landlord may have its financial benefits, but it's not for the faint of heart. Proceed cautiously!

Investment considerations for RIG #2: systematic withdrawals

If you've decided to use systematic withdrawals to generate your retirement paycheck, then you need more income than can be generated from interest and dividends alone. But be careful, because this drawdown method can resemble a high-wire, circus balancing act: Withdraw too rapidly or consistently realize poor investment returns, and sooner or later, your retirement savings will crash to the ground.

The worst possible scenario would be if you invest a significant portion of your retirement savings in stocks, withdraw from your retirement savings at an annual rate well above 4%, and then experience a stock market crash and/or high inflation early in your retirement, thus reducing your retirement savings more than you can afford. Various financial analysts and writers have repeatedly demonstrated that this scenario is likely to produce actuarial ruin; you'll end up not being able to make up for your losses, and you'll outlive your retirement savings.

But you can protect yourself against this unfortunate outcome by maintaining your asset allocation between the ranges I described previously in this chapter, withdrawing at a conservative rate (see Chapters 4 and 14 for more details on this), being vigilant about minimizing your investment management fees, and periodically resetting your withdrawal rate and rebalancing your portfolio.

You might think that the higher your allocation to stocks, the more vulnerable you are to stock market crashes and the higher your odds of ruin. But that's not necessarily the case. Wade Pfau, PhD, published an article in the *Journal of Financial Planning* titled "Capital Market Expectations, Asset Allocation, and Safe Withdrawal Rates." His analysis showed that the odds of ruin are roughly the same for portfolios invested anywhere within the range I described earlier (between one-third and two-thirds in stocks, with the rest in bonds and cash investments). You can expect a higher legacy value after you pass away, however, if you have a higher allocation to stocks. If you have a taste for financial analyses that support this conclusion, check out Dr. Pfau's article. You can find it on his blog by doing an Internet search on the title of the article.

Investment considerations for RIG #3: immediate annuities

If you'd like to minimize the number of investment decisions you'll need to make during your retirement, then RIG #3 (investing in immediate annuities) may be the route to take. You simply use part of your savings to buy an immediate fixed or inflation-adjusted annuity – or several annuities, depending on the amount you have in retirement savings. Then you're done making investment decisions on that part of your retirement savings and your retirement paycheck won't be vulnerable to stock market fluctuations.

If you buy an immediate variable annuity, as described previously in Chapter 5, then your retirement paycheck will increase or decrease to the extent that the return on the underlying investment portfolio is different from the assumed interest rate (AIR). Common AIRs are 3½% or 4%. If you invest in a portfolio that's balanced between stocks and bonds, there's a good chance that over the long run, your investments will beat these AIRs by one or two percentage points, giving you a nice boost in your retirement paycheck.

But there's always the possibility that a stocks and bonds portfolio will return less than the AIR, resulting in a decrease in your retirement paycheck. For example, in the 2008 - 2009 downturn, balanced portfolios experienced losses ranging from 10% to 25%. If the AIR of your immediate variable annuity had been 4%, you would have experienced *decreases* in your retirement paycheck of 14% to 29%, after reducing the return by the AIR. To recover from this drop in your retirement income, you'd need to earn back the drop in your retirement paycheck *plus* the AIR in each future year.

As we near publication of this book, the retirement values of many portfolios balanced between stocks and bonds have completely recovered the market losses they experienced in the 2008 - 2009 downturn. This performance, however, does not reflect the operation of the AIR; once you deduct the AIR for each year, the retirement income from many immediate variable annuities still hasn't recovered the full extent of the decrease in investors' monthly paychecks, due to the additional hurdle represented by the AIR.

I'm pointing all this out so that when you're considering an immediate variable annuity, you determine – before you invest – that you can tolerate decreases in your retirement paycheck of the magnitude shown above. These potential decreases are the price you pay for the potential growth in your retirement paycheck if investment returns are favorable.

If you're still interested in purchasing an immediate annuity, one other option to consider is a Guaranteed Lifetime Withdrawal Benefit (GLWB) product. As you'll see in Chapter 16, which goes into detail on this product, the retirement incomes generated by GLWBs are guaranteed not to decrease once benefits have started. It's also not likely, however, that you'll experience substantial increases in your retirement income. In effect, these products have AIRs that exceed 6%, meaning your portfolio would need to consistently beat 6% per year to produce any increases in your retirement income. Although it's possible that could happen in any given year, it's not likely to happen consistently over long periods of time.

Protecting yourself against market fluctuations

If you want a retirement paycheck that's 100% guaranteed not to decrease due to drops in the values of stocks or bonds, then you'll want to choose a fixed or inflation-adjusted immediate annuity, or one of the GLWB/GMWB hybrid insurance products I describe in Chapters 5 and 16. There's really no other way to *guarantee* a retirement income that's paid for the rest of your life and is immune from stock market fluctuations.

You can also use systematic withdrawals to generate a retirement paycheck with low odds of fluctuations in retirement income through a significant investment in bonds and a cautious initial withdrawal rate. One example of such a strategy is the service offered by Financial Engines' Income +, which is available in many large 401(k) plans.

Prudent ways to accept market risk

So how can you invest in stocks and other assets for the potential of growth in your retirement savings and retirement paycheck, without being vulnerable to uncomfortably large decreases in your retirement income?

Here are a few possibilities:

1. **Build a floor.** Buy an immediate fixed or inflation-adjusted annuity that, together with Social Security, will cover your basic living expenses. Then invest the balance of your savings in a low-cost index fund that's balanced between stocks and bonds, and use systematic withdrawals from this fund for the remainder of your retirement paycheck.

2. **Invest in a GLWB/GMWB product.** These products offer the potential for increases in your retirement income if the market does well. Unfortunately, you'll really need to generate significant returns in your underlying portfolio to achieve meaningful increases in your retirement income. See Chapter 16 for more details on this topic.

3. **Start low with systematic withdrawals.** If you just can't bring yourself to give any money to an insurance company by purchasing an immediate annuity or GLWB product, then invest in a low-cost index fund that's balanced between stocks and bonds. Keep your allocation to stocks between one-third and two-thirds of your portfolio. You could use a 50/50 split to keep your life simple or invest in a low-cost balanced mutual fund, such as Vanguard's Wellesley (40% stocks), Balanced Index (60% stocks), or Wellington (65% stocks) funds.

   Then start with a low, initial withdrawal rate – say 3½% and definitely no higher than 4%. Keep the withdrawal amount fixed in dollar terms for a few years. Then, if you've experience favorable returns for this period, adjust your withdrawals using the strategies I described in Chapters 4, 7, and 14.

I encourage you to read additional books and articles on retirement investing if you're interested in learning more about investing strategies. Some of my favorite online sources are the blogs of Dr. Wade Pfau, Allan Roth, Larry Swedroe, and Joe Tomlinson; you can find them by doing an Internet search on their names. As with all the other topics in this book, it's a good use of your time to learn as much as you can about managing your investment risk during retirement.

CHAPTER 14

Refining Your Strategy for Systematic Withdrawals

In Chapter 4, I introduced you to the complexities of determining a "safe" withdrawal rate when using the second retirement income generator (RIG), systematic withdrawals. If you're using this RIG, you're trying to cautiously draw down both your principal and your investment income to avoid outliving your savings.

What you learned is that the best withdrawal rate is a "Goldilocks" solution – not too high so that you outlive your money and not too low so that you restrain your retirement spending too much and leave behind a lot of money when you pass away. Of course, this goal is much easier said than done, because of the uncertainties surrounding the actual investment returns your retirement savings will earn and how long you'll live.

This chapter provides you with practical tips on how you can determine a withdrawal strategy that works for you, whether you're determining it yourself or working with an experienced financial advisor.

First, though, let me be blunt: The moment you begin to withdraw principal, you run the risk of outliving your money. You can minimize this risk with your withdrawal and investment strategies, but there will always be a risk that your money will expire before you do.

And since I'm being blunt, let me add one more thing: You may encounter financial advisors, experts, or analysts who may sound very convincing about their "safe" withdrawal strategy. They don't really know for sure that it will work, however, and they can't *absolutely guarantee* that your money will last as long as you do. The only time you'll know for sure that you've succeeded with a systematic withdrawal strategy is when you're on your deathbed with money left in the bank. Advisors with expertise and integrity should inform you of the risks and discuss strategies for *minimizing* the odds of actuarial ruin. But if they say they can *guarantee* you won't run out of money with systematic withdrawals, they're either fooling you, fooling themselves, or both.

You can get a wide range of opinions on a safe withdrawal rate from well-respected analysts. I've heard one analyst say that a safe annual withdrawal rate for a 30-year retirement for someone who is very cautious would be just 1.8%, while another qualified expert claims someone who's comfortable taking some risk – willing to put up with a 50/50 chance of actuarial ruin – could apply an annual withdrawal rate of 7%.

The smartest thing to do with systematic withdrawals is to start with a withdrawal rate that's appropriate for your circumstances and goals, and then periodically adjust the withdrawal rate – up or down – to reflect events that have happened since you last determined the withdrawal rate.

Any withdrawal strategy is based on making assumptions about how long you'll live and the investment returns you'll experience during your retirement. You may have heard of the acronym GIGO – "garbage in, garbage out" – when people talk about financial projections from any computer program. It's the same with making assumptions about investment returns and your longevity – any forecast is just as good as the assumptions that are used as input. The trouble is, you won't know if your assumptions have been the right ones until the very end.

For example, the well-used "four percent rule" is based on the assumption that you'll need a retirement income for 30 years and that you have substantial investments in stocks with an investment goal of outpacing inflation. If you retire much earlier than age 65, then a 4% withdrawal rate might be too high, since there's a good chance you might need an income for more than 30 years. On the other hand, if you retire much later than age 65, you might be able to use a withdrawal rate higher than 4%, since there could be a good chance you'll need the money for less than 30 years.

The four percent rule may also be too high if your retirement savings earns a rate of return that doesn't outpace inflation. For example, if all the money you have in retirement savings earns the same interest rate that savings accounts are earning in 2012 – nearly zero – your retirement savings won't earn you enough to support a 4% withdrawal rate.

Although systematic withdrawals may sound too hard to implement, they're not, and I'm not trying to discourage you from using this method to generate your retirement paycheck. Instead, I encourage you to do your homework and move ahead with a decision, knowing that you're doing the best you can. An important part of "doing the best you can" is choosing a withdrawal percentage that works for you at the time you retire, and then revisiting it periodically throughout your retirement.

To help you decide just how much money you can afford to withdraw each month, I'll describe three ways you can determine your withdrawal strategy:

1. The "deterministic" method, which involves making a single set of assumptions
2. The "Monte Carlo" method, in which you estimate the chances of failure for different withdrawal and investment strategies, based on a model that predicts future asset returns on various types of investments
3. The "historical" method, which ensures you could have survived every possible investment period by reviewing investment histories for stocks, bonds, and cash investments that are available and appropriate for your circumstances

Deterministic method

The first method you can use for choosing a withdrawal strategy is called a "deterministic" method, since the assumptions you make about how much money you'll need, how long you'll need it, and what the market will do will determine a single projected retirement income.

Many experts have developed their own deterministic methods, including my good friend, Ken Steiner, who recently retired from the prestigious actuarial and consulting firm Towers Watson, where he was in charge of the company's actuarial research department. Finding out how an actuary determines a withdrawal strategy is somewhat like discovering what a credentialed nutritionist eats: You can learn a lot just by finding out what an expert does for himself or herself.

Over the years, Steiner gave a lot of thought to the challenge of generating a lifetime retirement income, and he invented a simple tool that builds on his substantial experience with analyzing retirement programs. He used this tool to help with his own retirement, and now he's sharing it with others through his website, *How Much Can I Afford to Spend in Retirement*. It contains a simple retirement income calculator along with text that describes his approach and provides instructions on how to use the calculator.

To use Steiner's calculator, you'll need to make a few key assumptions about your future:

- how many years you'll be retired and will need retirement income (your expected length of retirement),
- the rate at which your retirement nest egg will grow, considering both appreciation and income, and
- your expected inflation rate or, in other words, what percentage you need your retirement income to increase each year to cover the cost of your living expenses.

In addition, you'll need to know the current value of your retirement savings from all sources.

Once you input all this information, Steiner's program calculates how much you can safely withdraw for the coming year. The amount is generated in such a way that if all the above assumptions exactly match your actual future experience regarding investment return and inflation, your money will run out by the end of your (expected) life.

Since you can't count on your assumptions to exactly match what will happen in the future, however, each year you should recalculate your withdrawal amount for the following year and, if necessary, make adjustments in your assumptions. Most important, you'll update the amount that remains in your retirement savings. And you'll do this every year during your retirement in order to make sure that you're withdrawing enough to cover your expenses, but are also leaving enough so you can continue to generate enough income to last throughout your retirement.

This constant adjustment of the withdrawal amount is one of the advantages of Steiner's method. By recalculating this amount each year, you have a greater chance of not outliving your savings. A pure application of the four percent rule, on the other hand, locks you into a fixed withdrawal amount without recognizing what's happened to your investments. This doesn't make sense to me.

The assumptions you input into Steiner's program are critical: If you're too optimistic about your investment return or if you live longer than your expected length of retirement, you can outlive your money. But you can minimize the odds of outliving your money by being conservative in your assumptions.

For your expected length of retirement, I'd use an online life expectancy calculator such as www.livingto100.com or www.bluezones.com – see Chapter 1 for details on these calculators. Then I'd add five years to the result, just to be safe. If you're married or in a committed relationship, you should estimate your spouse or partner's life expectancy as well. Then each year before you recalculate your withdrawal amount, you should revisit the online life expectancy calculator to reflect what's happened in your life since the previous year.

If this is too much calculating for you, a simpler approach would be to simply assume you'll need retirement income until your 95th birthday or your spouse's 95th birthday, whichever is later. Of course, this assumption won't make sense as you approach your 90s, since the closer you get to age 95, the greater the odds you'll live beyond that age. You may want to start adjusting this assumption if you live into your late 80s.

Your assumption regarding the rate of return on your retirement savings should reflect your asset allocation. You might want to be a bit conservative here to make sure you don't outlive your retirement savings. For instance, for a balanced portfolio invested in stocks and bonds, I'd assume an annual rate of 5% or 6% (even though Monte Carlo and other analyses might produce higher expected rates, such as 7%).

When it comes to inflation, an annual rate of 2½% to 3½% seems reasonable to me, though you could use 4% if you want to be cautious or are pessimistic.

The table below shows annual withdrawal rates produced by Steiner's program using a retirement period of 30 years, assuming a few different scenarios for investment returns and inflation. Table 14.1 shows that these forecasts produce withdrawal rates in the neighborhood of 4% for a "real" rate of return (your total rate of return minus the inflation rate) somewhere between 1% and 2%; these real returns are somewhat conservative for a portfolio invested as described in Chapter 13.

TABLE 14.1 WITHDRAWAL PERCENTAGES FOR VARIOUS ECONOMIC ASSUMPTIONS

Assumed return on savings	Assumed inflation rate	Real rate of return	Withdrawal percentage
4%	3%	1%	3.8%
5%	3%	2%	4.3%
5%	4%	1%	3.8%
6%	4%	2%	4.3%
7%	4%	3%	4.9%

The main advantage of using Steiner's approach is that you adjust your withdrawal amount each year, reflecting the latest value of your retirement savings and how many years remain for which you expect to need retirement income.

One word of warning: You should be prepared to reduce your retirement income if your investments perform poorly; this will help your retirement savings withstand a market downturn. On the other hand, if your investments perform better than expected, you could choose to increase your withdrawal amount.

Steiner's website also contains an optional algorithm for smoothing out your withdrawals from year to year when resetting your withdrawal amount. To smooth out your withdrawals, you would choose not to increase or decrease your withdrawal amount to the full extent suggested by his calculator. You'd do this if you think your investments are either temporarily depressed or overvalued at the time you're resetting your withdrawals.

Steiner's calculator has a few more nifty features:

- If you want to leave a legacy with money from your retirement savings, the calculator allows you to reduce your withdrawal rate accordingly by specifying the amount of legacy you desire to leave.
- If you have a fixed pension from your work or a fixed annuity, the calculator can tell you how much additional money you should withdraw to give yourself cost of living increases on this fixed monthly paycheck.

You can find Ken Steiner's online calculator, along with an excellent paper describing his method, by doing an Internet search on the phrase "How much can I afford to spend in retirement." There are other online programs similar to Steiner's that assume single fixed rates for your asset return and inflation and for a fixed number of remaining years of life.

If you decide to use a deterministic calculator, I recommend you run the projections several times, each time varying such factors as projected investment returns, projected withdrawal rates from your retirement savings, projected inflation rates, how long you expect to live, and your retirement age. By changing these numbers, you'll see how sensitive the results are to the assumptions you make.

Remember – a main goal of this effort is to help you survive future downturns. This means you should project what will happen to your financial situation assuming that such downturns will occur in the future. Many smart decision-makers – including presidents and generals – use this type of "scenario planning" system to evaluate their options and make informed decisions after taking a number of factors into account. Knowing what could happen in your future will help you put strategies in place to protect your assets.

The best advice I can give you is this: Give yourself peace of mind by planning for the worst, and then enjoy life if the worst doesn't happen.

Monte Carlo method

Some retirement calculators use sophisticated techniques called "Monte Carlo" forecasts, also known as "stochastic" projections. These calculators run 500 or more simulations of the future under a variety of possible future economic scenarios regarding rates of return and inflation, and then calculate the odds of you outliving your retirement savings.

Monte Carlo calculators build in a number of assumptions regarding the rate of inflation and investment returns on various types of assets, including stocks, bonds, and cash. They also make assumptions on the possible variation in these returns and attempt to mimic reality by building in some randomness in the projected returns. These assumptions are typically constructed by looking at historical rates of returns, and then making adjustments for how future returns might be different from historical returns, based on the judgment of the people constructing the program.

One popular Monte Carlo calculator can be found on the T. Rowe Price website. You can find it easily by conducting an Internet search on the keyword phrase "retirement income calculator T Rowe Price."

With the T. Rowe Price system, you enter such personal information as:

- your date of birth,
- the date of birth of your spouse or partner,
- your account balances,
- the asset allocation on your retirement savings, and
- your guess at an initial annual amount you want to withdraw from your savings or, said another way, your estimate of the amount of your retirement living expenses that you want to pay from your retirement savings.

The calculator will also ask you how much income you expect to receive from Social Security and from a pension, if you'll be getting one. If you just want to focus on a withdrawal strategy for your retirement savings instead of planning your total retirement income from all sources, you can enter zero for both Social Security and pension incomes. For your living expenses, you can enter just the annual amount you hope to withdraw from your retirement savings, not your total living expenses in retirement.

Using the withdrawal amount you entered, the calculator will then tell you the odds of your retirement savings lasting until you reach age 95 (or until your spouse or partner reaches age 95, if that's later than the time you'll reach it). It will also tell you the withdrawal amount that offers a 90% chance of your retirement savings lasting until age 95. Depending on the results you get, you can always recalculate the odds by adjusting a few input items, such as your expected withdrawal amount, your asset allocation, or how long you want your savings to last.

Here's an example of the results produced by the T. Rowe Price system in mid-2012 for a 65-year-old couple with retirement savings invested 60% in stocks, 30% in bonds, and 10% in cash. With a 4% withdrawal rate, the calculator predicted that the couple's retirement savings would have a 78% chance of lasting until age 95. If this couple wanted a 90% chance of success, they'd need to reduce their annual withdrawal rate to 3.3%.

While the output of a Monte Carlo system appears to be very sophisticated, it's important to remember that it's a system that works by making a lot of assumptions based on the judgment of the professionals who built the system. I've seen some very qualified and experienced professionals have serious disagreements on the appropriate assumptions for Monte Carlo forecasts, and the results of their forecasts can vary widely.

If you use a Monte Carlo system, I suggest that you focus on the results that minimize your odds of failure, say one out of 10. To generate these results, you'd need to withdraw according to a forecast that had a 90% success rate – often called a "90% confidence level."

Now you may think that's being too conservative and you'd prefer to withdraw from your retirement savings the amounts associated with a 50% success rate. According to the T. Rowe Price system, you'd now have a 50/50 chance of outliving your retirement savings. Those aren't very good odds for such an unpleasant outcome.

I also believe that even the most sophisticated Monte Carlo system can't accurately predict the timing and magnitude of "rare" events such as a market meltdown. Is the chance of a future meltdown 1%, 5%, 10%, or 20%? I contend that these systems can't refine the odds this accurately; instead, the best we can reliably say is that these events don't happen very often, but when they do, you could be in trouble, so be prepared.

Historical method

This third method for determining your withdrawal amount doesn't attempt to predict future returns as the basis for a withdrawal strategy, like the first two methods described above. Instead, it shows how your withdrawal strategy would have worked during all possible prior periods of time, considering your asset allocation and the historical returns on various asset classes. This is the approach used by William Bengen, the financial planner who developed the four percent rule, as described in Chapter 4.

According to this method, if your withdrawal strategy would have survived the worst possible investment periods in the past, then you can feel confident it will survive them in the future. The FIRECalc system is one of the best historical calculators I've seen; you can find it at www.firecalc.com.

Using FIRECalc's simplest application, you tell it:

- how much you have in retirement savings,
- how much you plan to withdraw in the first year, and
- the length of time you want your retirement income to last.

The calculator then shows you how your withdrawal strategy would have worked for all retirements starting in 1871 up to the present. It does this by graphing a line for each starting year of retirement and showing the projected amount of your retirement savings at each year, reflecting estimated withdrawals and assuming your investments would earn the historical rates of return each year. If a specific line falls below zero, that indicates a historical period in which your withdrawal strategy would have failed. To feel confident about a withdrawal strategy, you'll want to select a withdrawal strategy with few failures, or none at all. You can see this visually with the graphs produced by the FIRECalc system.

The initial output assumes that you'll increase your withdrawal amount for inflation each year according to the Consumer Price Index (CPI) and that your retirement savings are invested in a portfolio of 75% stock index and 25% bond funds, with a 0.18% (18 basis points) investment management fee. When I used the calculator, for this base scenario, it told me that a withdrawal rate of 4% would have failed in 6 out of 111 possible 30-year periods for an overall success rate of 94.6%.

The system lets you make many useful adjustments. For example, you can:

- change your asset allocation from the allocation automatically assumed by the system,
- give your retirement income increases that are different from the CPI,
- estimate the effect of paying fees higher than 18 basis points, either as investment management fees or if you pay a financial advisor from your retirement savings,
- estimate the effect of using different withdrawal strategies, or
- take into account possible legacy amounts you may wish to leave.

Like the other systems described above, you can factor in other sources of income, such as Social Security, if you want to project your retirement income from all sources to determine if your total paycheck will be adequate to cover your living expenses in retirement.

Comparing the three methods

Each of the three methods has its advantages and disadvantages, but it's interesting to note that they produce results that are in the same ballpark with respect to a 4% withdrawal rate for a 30-year retirement.

Critics of the deterministic method say that it's too simple and that it doesn't take into account alternative scenarios. But simplicity is the beauty of this method, and you do have the ability to input different assumptions to see the effect of alternative scenarios.

On the other hand, critics of the Monte Carlo method say that it's impossible to predict future returns and possible variations with certainty, and that the output is only as good as the assumptions you make. While that's true, you have to make some assumptions with any method.

Finally, critics of the historical method will say that there's always the possibility that the future may bring scenarios we haven't experienced before – they point to the 2011 earthquake in Japan as an event that fell outside of historical experience. Again, while that's true, such events may not show up in the other methods either.

No matter how simple or how sophisticated, all of the methods discussed above are based on making *some* assumptions about the future, and those assumptions could turn out to be wrong. But the fact is, you have to do something. Each method, properly used, can form the basis of a reasonable withdrawal strategy.

Just don't make the mistake of assuming that the economic model that supports your withdrawal method is infallible, and don't confuse the model with reality. The 2008 - 2009 stock market crash proved that very sophisticated economic models created by very smart people can be very wrong. The best thing you can do is to be prepared to make mid-course adjustments if your investment experience turns out to be different from the assumptions that are inherent in the method you use.

It's also a good idea to use more than one system, at least at the beginning of your retirement, and then compare the results. Try to understand the reasons for the differences, and then use the results from the system that make you feel the most comfortable. By using more than one system, you'll learn more about withdrawal strategies and will probably find it easier to make an informed decision. And, as I've mentioned before, be prepared to make mid-course adjustments throughout your retirement.

I also want to point out that I haven't completed an exhaustive study of all the methods and systems available for devising withdrawal strategies; reporting on such a study would make this a very long book! What I've done is described a few of the systems I've come across, ones that are readily available and free on the Internet. I'm sure there are other reasonable methods and systems out there, but some of those will be fee-based and I wanted to offer solutions that wouldn't cost you anything.

If you're not bothered by the idea of paying for help, then one of the most detailed online planners I've seen, available for purchase at www.Retirement-Works2.com, is called RW2 for YOU. In particular, I like that it projects your results using alternative future scenarios, which will help you understand how to withstand the risks of different possible economic and life events. It also offers a detailed action plan.

Leaving a legacy

Many people want to leave a legacy to their children or charities from their retirement savings. The deterministic and historical systems described above both allow you to estimate how much you'll want to reduce your withdrawal amounts so you can leave a specified legacy. This is one way to add in a safety margin in your withdrawal strategy. If you plan for leaving a certain amount of a legacy, and if your investments perform poorly or you live a long time, the projected legacy can be a reserve you can tap for needed retirement income. On the other hand, if your investments perform well, you can still pass on the legacy.

Given the modest level of the retirement savings most boomers have managed to accumulate, leaving a meaningful legacy from retirement savings may not be practical. Most Americans will need to generate as much retirement income as possible; in fact, the legacy they should try to avoid is the need to move in with their children if their money runs out!

If you don't think you'll have enough money in retirement savings to leave any portion of it as a legacy, you can still leave a legacy from other assets, such as your home equity, jewelry, furniture, and so on. Such a legacy is possible even if you buy an annuity that leaves no wealth when you pass away.

For more homework

If you want to learn more about potential withdrawal strategies, two sources that I respect and that offer additional information are the online blogs of Wade Pfau, PhD, associate professor of economics at the National Graduate Institute for Policy Studies in Tokyo and curriculum director for the Retirement Income Industry Association, and Joe Tomlinson, an actuary and financial planner. I've met both of them and found them to be sincerely dedicated to improving our understanding of the best methods to generate retirement income from your savings.

Both Dr. Pfau and Tomlinson write for journals read by financial advisors, and their articles contain detailed analyses and charts on withdrawal strategies. On their blogs, you'll see they've covered such interesting subjects as:

- the effects of combining annuities with systematic withdrawals,
- how using different investment histories will impact a withdrawal strategy,
- how combining different asset classes affects a withdrawal strategy,
- how various withdrawal strategies would have worked in other countries,
- how you can use different methods of "flooring" to protect necessary retirement spending, and
- thoughts on leaving a legacy.

One of the most important subjects they've both covered is how to adjust your withdrawal strategy considering the economic climate in effect in 2012 (very low interest rates on bonds and savings accounts). Many analysts believe we may be in a period that's not reflected in the historical record on investments and that most of the historical record is based on a remarkable period in U.S. history. If you believe this is the case, you should reduce the amount you withdraw compared to withdrawal amounts that are supported by the historical record.

You can find either of these expert's blogs by doing an Internet search on their names.

Working with financial advisors

If you're working with a financial advisor, be sure to ask them about the method and system they use to determine a safe withdrawal strategy and the reasons they use that particular approach. You may even want to ask them to use one of the methods described here in addition to the approach they recommend, just to double-check the strategy they recommend.

And if you really want to be thorough, get a second opinion from another financial planner. Second opinions are common with high-stakes medical decisions, such as major surgery; your withdrawal strategy is just as important and deserves the same level of due diligence.

Don't feel shy about making these requests of a potential financial advisor. After all, if you outlive your retirement savings, you'll be the one to suffer the consequences – not your financial advisor. A good advisor won't feel threatened by these requests and will most likely be glad to talk about their methods and tools, and discuss the pros and cons of different approaches.

Remember, it's your life and your money. If you decide to use systematic withdrawals to generate your retirement paycheck, take the time to do the job right. It will take many hours to do the homework advocated in this chapter, but that's appropriate given that you're planning your financial security for the rest of your life. You'll sleep better knowing you're doing the best you can.

CHAPTER 15

•••••

Protecting Your Annuity

If you're reading this chapter, you're probably considering using some form of annuity to generate your retirement paycheck. Congratulations for hanging in there and having the determination to learn more!

This chapter focuses on one of the primary concerns people have when purchasing an annuity: What happens if the insurance company you purchased your annuity from fails? Will you lose everything, or will your money be safe?

The well-publicized failure of many banks during the recent economic downturn has only exacerbated people's fears of insurance company bankruptcy. Some people are so worried about the possibility that the insurance company might fail and they might lose their retirement savings in the process that they decide not to purchase any type of annuity, eliminating one of the best ways to generate a retirement income.

So is this issue something that should prevent you from buying an annuity? Probably not, but you'll want to pay attention to the details in order to make sure you understand exactly what you're buying.

There are three important things you need to know before you purchase an annuity from an insurance company:

1. **State guaranty associations protect your policy.** There's no federal program in place that protects consumers from insurance company bankruptcies similar to the Federal Deposit Insurance Corporation (FDIC) that protects consumers against bank failures. However, each state does have an insurance guaranty association (GA) that backs up insurance company policies in the event of the insurance company's bankruptcy. Your state's GA is funded from

the assessments it charges every insurance company that currently does business in your state. This money pays for the obligations of any failed insurance company that had been approved by your state's GA to conduct business in your state.

If your insurance company should fail, your policy is most likely protected by the GA in your state of residence, even if you bought the policy while living in another state. In some cases, the protection may be provided by the state where the insurance company had its headquarters.

As with FDIC insurance, there's a limit to the amount of insurance protection offered by a GA. This limit varies by state and depends on the type of insurance you have. For example, common insurance limits are $300,000 for life insurance death benefits, $100,000 for cash surrender values of life insurance policies, and $100,000 or $250,000 for annuity contracts. You can learn more about the terms, including the limits of protection for annuities, that apply in your state of residence at the website of the National Organization of Life & Health Insurance Guaranty Associations (NOLHGA). This website also contains a link to each state's guaranty association.

2. **Insurance company failures are different from bank failures.** Although bank failures have caused people to be concerned about the stability of all financial institutions, it's important to recognize the critical differences between failures of banks and failures of insurance companies. Below are some key differences.

   It's hard to start a "run" on an insurance company like a "run" on a bank. While customers can always withdraw money from their bank accounts, customers can't typically withdraw money they paid to an insurance company for a policy or annuity. Once you've paid for a policy, you have to die for any life insurance benefits to be paid; with an immediate annuity, you have to wait each month to receive your check. In most cases, you can't get the money back just because you want it.

   Insurance companies aren't usually as leveraged as banks are, so when they fail, their liabilities are more likely to be just 10% to 20% higher than their assets. A bank's liabilities, on the other hand, can be far higher than its assets.

   As a result of these differences, there have been far fewer insurance company failures compared to bank failures. According to the most recent report from the NOLHGA, between 1987 and 2009, there were 74 failures of multi-state insurance companies that the NOLHGA was involved with. By contrast, there were 157 bank failures in 2010 alone, and another 92 in 2011.

3. **Separate accounts can provide additional protection**. Most fixed and inflation-adjusted annuities are protected by the general assets of the insurance company from which you bought the annuity. In these cases, the guarantees described above are your only protection if the insurance company goes bankrupt.

   On the other hand, some variable annuities invest your contributions in separate accounts, which are then held in a trust that's separate from the general assets of the insurance company. These accounts may be protected from creditors in the event the insurance company goes bankrupt, and they can provide an additional layer of protection.

So what can you do to be certain your assets are as safe as possible? There are two steps you can take to protect yourself from insurance company failures. First, learn about the limits of your state's guaranty association, and then keep your annuity purchases below this limit. To do this, you may need to buy annuities from more than one insurance company.

Second, only buy annuities from the top-rated insurance companies. You can determine an insurance company's ratings if you use one of the online annuity bidding services mentioned in Chapter 5, such as Hueler's Income Solutions or ImmediateAnnuities.com.

Since it's likely you'll be receiving annuity payments for a long period of time – and it's important to be able to rely on your annuity paycheck – I suggest you only work with insurance companies that have one of the top four ratings assigned by insurance rating companies such as A. M. Best, Moody's, or Standard & Poor's. The top four ratings from these services are described as "superior," "extremely strong," "exceptional," "excellent," or "very strong." Table 15.1 shows the top four ratings from the above-mentioned rating companies.

TABLE 15.1 TOP FOUR INSURANCE COMPANY RATINGS

Rating company	Top four ratings
A. M. Best	A++, A+, A, A-
Moody's	Aaa or Aa1, Aa2, Aa3
Standard & Poor's	AAA, AA+, AA, AA-

Some critics of annuities raise the scenario of a catastrophic economic failure of our financial system, where insurance companies go bankrupt and state guaranty associations can't back up their promises. While it's certainly possible that could happen, such an event would also devastate most other investments these critics suggest you buy instead. If the thought of this scenario happening really bothers you, bury some gold or diamonds in your backyard; throughout history, that's how people in other times and places have salvaged their wealth during political upheavals and economic disasters. You could also put a stash of cash in U.S. treasury bonds, but if the catastrophic event really takes place, these might be in jeopardy as well.

The bottom line is, you should not let the fear of insurance company failure hold you back from being able to generate a secure, lifetime retirement income. If you do your homework, you can minimize your exposure to the potential bankruptcy of your insurance company.

CHAPTER 16

A Closer Look at Guaranteed Lifetime Withdrawal Benefits

In Chapter 5, I briefly described a set of hybrid annuity products offered by a few insurance companies and mutual fund companies that combine the best features of systematic withdrawals with the guarantee of a lifetime retirement income. These products most commonly go by two names: guaranteed lifetime withdrawal benefits (GLWB) or guaranteed minimum withdrawal benefits (GMWB). For the sake of simplification, I'll use the term GLWB in this chapter for short.

To help you determine whether these products might be a good way for you to generate retirement income given your particular goals and circumstances, this chapter offers more details on these complex products.

The basics

Let's briefly review the fundamentals of these "annuities with a twist": With this type of annuities, you have the guarantee of a fixed lifetime income with the upside potential for growth in both your retirement savings and your retirement income if the stock market does well. You also have a guarantee that your savings or income won't decrease if the stock market crashes.

Unlike conventional immediate annuities, however, you can cancel the annuity and withdraw the remaining part of your retirement savings at any time after you've invested in these products, even after your retirement income starts. Finally, any unused funds at your death can provide a financial legacy.

But all these features come at a cost: In addition to the usual investment management fees, your retirement savings are assessed an annual insurance charge of 1% or more of your retirement savings for the "guarantee" that your money will never lose its value. As a result, you'll most likely receive an income over your lifetime that's lower than what you'd get from a traditional fixed annuity, and you'll leave a lower legacy than if you had chosen to use a systematic withdrawal approach.

Do these products sound too good to be true? They're not. But should you consider investing your retirement savings in them? Possibly, but there's a price you'll have to pay to have your cake and eat it, too, though many people might find the price easy to swallow. Let's dig into the details so you can evaluate these products for yourself.

Because GLWBs can be used both for accumulating savings before retirement and for generating a lifetime paycheck during retirement, I'll first review how GLWBs work during the accumulation phase, and then I'll examine the retirement phase.

Accumulation before retirement

If you decide to use a GLWB, you'll typically invest your retirement savings in one of a handful of funds that offer different allocations among stocks and bonds. The funds are often target date funds in which the asset allocation to stocks starts at levels ranging from 70% to 90% and declines to 50% to 60% as you approach retirement.

The institution from which you purchase the GLWB accumulates an amount that's typically called the "income base," "benefit value," "guaranteed value," or "withdrawal value"; again, for the sake of simplification, I'll use the term "income base" throughout this chapter. The income base is the amount of money or "value" that's eventually used to generate a lifetime paycheck for you when you retire. This value is increased by the amount of your contributions and the earnings on your investments, and it's decreased by any of the expenses on the product, including investment management expenses and the charge for the guarantees.

Typically the institution guarantees that the income base will never drop below the value of your accumulated contributions, or the value that exists when you elect to start the GLWB guarantees. In addition, many policies will also lock in accumulated investment gains as well. Each product offers different income base guarantees that are described in the policy's fine print. I strongly advise that while you should read and understand the entire policy, you should pay particular attention to the income base guarantees before you invest.

In the accumulation phase, you typically don't start using the GLWB guarantees or paying for their charges until five to 10 years before you expect to retire; the assumption is that in the years leading up to your retirement, you'll value the protection against downside risk for your account. If you're 10 or more years away from retirement, the assumption is that you'll have enough time to recover from a stock market downturn, so you don't need to pay for the downside protection on your account.

Watch out for surrender value charges

The "surrender value" is the amount of money you're allowed to withdraw from the account at any time; with many GLWB products, the surrender value doesn't necessarily equal the income base, and in fact, it's often less. It's possible that the surrender value won't be subject to the same guarantees as the income base or that there's a surrender charge that's deducted from the income base to determine your surrender value. Once again, the method of calculating the surrender value is spelled out in the policy's fine print, which you should read so that you'll understand just what will happen with your investment if you should choose to withdraw some or all of it.

GLWB products are often sold with the convincing pitch that "you can always withdraw your money if you change your mind." These guarantees won't mean much, however, if the fine print shows that the surrender value is much less than the income base. Before you invest any money in a GLWB product, take the time to learn how the surrender value is calculated and whether it's likely to be much less than the income base.

Learn about the guarantees

During the accumulation phase and while the insurance guarantees are in place, GLWBs offer protection against the value of your retirement savings declining in the years approaching your retirement due to a stock market decline or a rise in interest rates, with upside potential if stock and bond markets do well. The most cost-effective GLWB products charge about 1% of the income base each year for the guarantee. I recommend that you only use GLWB products that assess insurance charges at or below 1% and avoid products with charges well above 1%. Note that I'm only talking about the insurance guarantee; you'll also have to pay investment management expenses on top of the insurance fee, and you'll want to look for products that minimize those fees as well.

Is it worth paying for the GLWB insurance guarantees? It can be. But let's look at an example that can help you think clearly about the risk and return tradeoff of this product to see how this might play out.

Suppose you're 10 years away from retirement and are trying to decide whether to keep your retirement savings in a target date fund without any GLWB protection or to add the GLWB protection. As I mentioned above, the best GLWB products typically charge about 1% of your income base each year for the downside protection on your retirement savings. In essence, your net return each year will be about 1% less with the GLWB protection than without the GLWB protection.

In this example, with the GLWB protection, your income base would be charged 1% each year for 10 years. So the income base with the GLWB protection at the end of the 10-year period would be about 10% less than if you had simply invested in the target date fund without the GLWB protection – ignoring for the moment the GLWB protection. (Because of compounding and the exact application of the insurance guarantee, the difference could be a little different, but 10% is close enough for this example.) Remember, though, that your income base with the GLWB protection can also never decrease during this period.

Figure 16.1 contains a simplified example that compares the total change in your account values with and without the GLWB protection for various rates of total appreciation or depreciation during the 10 years in our example.

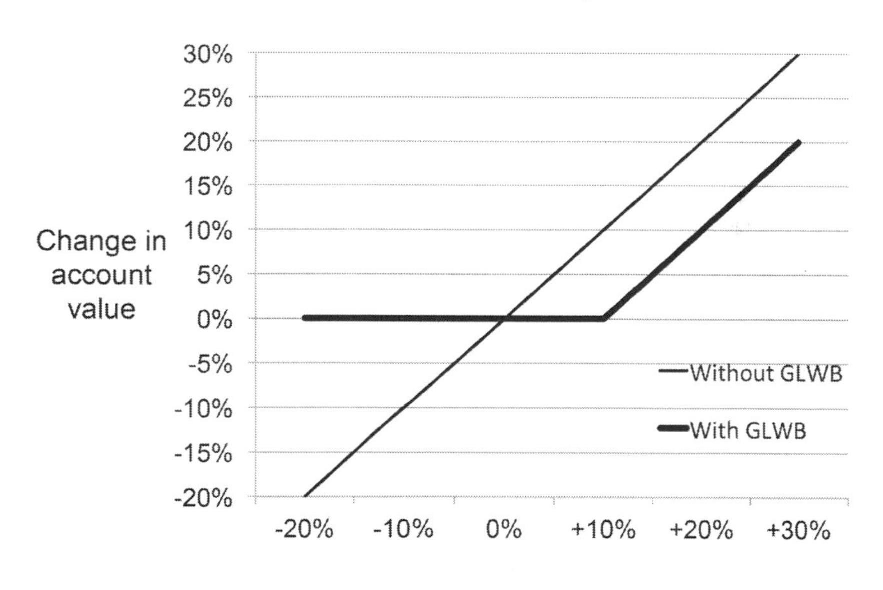

FIGURE 16.1 SIMPLE EXAMPLE OF GLWB PROTECTION

Now let's say the target date fund that your money is invested in appreciates by about 20% over the course of those 10 years. If that's the case, then your retirement savings would be 20% higher for the unprotected account but only about 10% higher for the income base with the GLWB protection (20% return minus about 10% for the guarantee fees). But what if your target date fund loses 20% of its value over those 10 years? Then you'd be 20% poorer with an unprotected account. But that wouldn't be the case if you had GLWB protection because your income base wouldn't drop at all.

Note that this simplified example ignores the order of the years in which you earn your gains or losses, and it simplifies the compounding of investment returns and the guarantee fees. Some GLWB products lock in accumulated gains each year, so it's possible that the difference between accumulations with and without GLWB protection could be different than laid out in Figure 16.1. Nevertheless, this example illustrates how GLWBs provide absolute downside protection, but the price is that your account forgoes some upside potential.

Do you really need to pay for peace of mind?

Many financial advisors claim that the odds are low that you'll ever need the protection a GLWB product offers, and they may have extensive analyses to support their position. But let's dig a little deeper and consider the behavioral finance aspects that affect your investing decision.

People who were invested in target date or balanced funds just before the 2008 - 2009 meltdown experienced 20% to 30% declines in their retirement savings in less than a year. This financially devastated many people who were a few years away from retirement, and many people had to postpone their retirement plans. Even worse, many people bailed out of their target date or balanced funds because they were afraid the values would keep dropping.

So would it have been worth it for these people to avoid these declines by giving up some upside potential with the GLWB protection? It's easy to imagine many people answering "yes" to this question.

Before deciding on your answer, it's important to point out that by the fall of 2011 – three years after the crash – many balanced portfolios had recovered all their losses. So if you had had the stomach to maintain your asset allocation, in this situation, you might have had to postpone your retirement by as little as three years.

It turns out that the real losers of the 2008 - 2009 downturn were the people who bailed out of their target date or balanced funds and moved all their assets into "safe" CDs or money market funds, which, as of 2012, were earning a piddly amount of interest. These investors missed the significant stock market rally that followed the crash – if they had only remained invested, they most likely would have recouped their losses by now.

This scenario illustrates the value offered by GLWB products during the final years of the accumulation phase: If they give you the peace of mind and the confidence to stay invested in target date or balanced funds, it might be worth paying the price of the GLWB guarantees. On the other hand, if you have the stomach to ride out stock market declines or are able to postpone your retirement by a few years if there's a stock market crash during the few years before you plan to retire, then you might not need to pay for GLWB protection.

If you decide you want GLWB protection, the example of the 2008 - 2009 crash suggests you might not need the GLWB protection until about five years before your retirement, since the odds are very good that you could ride out a stock market drop that's more than five years prior to your expected retirement. Note that with most GLWB policies, you can elect when to start the protection and pay the guarantee fees. You could decide to forgo paying GLWB fees until five years before you retire, creating an income base that would be about 5% higher when you eventually retire, compared to electing the GLWB coverage for the 10 years prior to your retirement. Another strategy would be to start paying the guarantee fee after the market has run up to "lock in" your account value.

If your head is spinning by now, don't give up! It's worth it to spend the time to assess whether these sophisticated products are appropriate for your situation and your tolerance for investment risk. The upside could be worth it.

Now let's look at GLWBs in the retirement phase.

Generating income in retirement

During your retirement, you'll continue to keep your retirement savings invested in a portfolio that's allocated between stocks and bonds; this is often – and conveniently – done through a target date fund that's appropriate for retirees. Asset allocations to stocks typically range from 50% to 60%, with the remainder in bonds or cash investments.

To generate retirement income, you'll apply the GLWB policy's maximum withdrawal percentage to the income base to determine the amount of your annual retirement income. The withdrawal percentage that applies to you typically depends on your age and whether the income will be continued to your spouse or partner after you die. For example, Table 16.1 shows the maximum withdrawal rates in 2012 for Prudential's IncomeFlex GLWB product.

TABLE 16.1 PRUDENTIAL'S INCOMEFLEX 2012 MAXIMUM WITHDRAWAL RATES

Age when withdrawals start	Maximum annual withdrawal percentage for a single person	Maximum annual withdrawal percentage for a couple
55 - 64	4.25%	3.75%
65 - 69	5.00%	4.50%
70+	5.75%	5.25%

Using the numbers in Table 16.1, let's determine how you'd fare if you and your spouse were both age 65 when you retired and your income base was $100,000. Your policy's withdrawal percentage would be 4.5%, and your initial retirement income would be $4,500 per year, or $375 per month. (The maximum withdrawal percentages in 2012 for other GLWB products are similar to the numbers shown in Table 16.1 for Prudential's IncomeFlex.)

You typically lock in your withdrawal percentage when you start your benefits. So if the withdrawal percentages are similar to the numbers in Table 16.1, it would be a good idea to start your retirement income when you're at the bottom of an age bracket. For example, you wouldn't want to start benefits at age 64, when one year later, the withdrawal percentage increases. Be sure to read the policy's fine print to understand how your withdrawal percentage is determined and whether it's locked in once you start making withdrawals.

During your retirement, the income base will continue to be increased for investment earnings, and decreased by investment expenses and the insurance company's charges for the guarantees, just as they were in the accumulation phase. In addition, the income base will be decreased by the amount of your withdrawals for retirement income. Periodically – typically annually – the withdrawal percentage will be reapplied to the income base, and if the income base at the time is higher than your previous income base, your retirement income will increase. This gives some potential for your retirement income to increase if your funds perform well.

If the stock or bond markets decline, however, remember that your retirement income will never decrease below the amount of your initial retirement income (provided you don't withdraw more than the amounts specified in the policy that trigger the surrender charges). This income amount is guaranteed for the rest of your life and that of your spouse or partner, if you elect to cover your beneficiary.

If there's still a positive value in your savings when you die (and after your spouse or partner dies, if you've elected a joint life policy), then this amount will be paid to your designated beneficiary or charity. This amount is often the market value of your savings without the guarantees on your account, not the income base that reflects the guarantees. Once again, the fine print will spell out how any death benefit is calculated.

With these products, you are allowed to withdraw more than the amount dictated by the maximum withdrawal percentage, but that will reduce the amount of your future monthly retirement income and may reduce or eliminate your lifetime guaranteed income. Once again, the policy's fine print will spell out how the policy calculates the income base, surrender value, and guaranteed retirement income once your retirement paycheck starts.

Understand how the fees work

The best GLWB products will charge a total of 150 to 200 basis points (from 1.5% to 2%) each year for any investment management expenses and the insurance guarantee. These charges would be applied to your income base during the year and are used to carry forward your income base to the next year.

For example, in 2012, Prudential's IncomeFlex product charged:

- 1% each year for the insurance guarantee, plus
- investment management and administrative expenses that ranged from 0.59% to 0.94%, depending on the fund an investor chose.

Adding these fees together results in total annual charges that range from 1.59% to 1.94%. Similar to most GLWB providers, Prudential reserves the right to increase the 1% insurance charge to as much as 1.5% for future contributions and for future step-ups in the income base.

Similarly, in 2012, the Vanguard Variable Annuity with the GLWB rider charged:

- 0.95% each year for the insurance guarantee, plus
- investment management and administrative expenses that ranged from 0.47% to 0.81%, depending on the fund an investor chose.

Adding these fees together results in total annual charges that range from 1.42% to 1.76%. Vanguard reserves the right to increase its 0.95% insurance charge to as much as 2%.

It's important to point out that some retail GLWB products can have total charges well above 200 basis points (2%), with some reaching as high as 300 basis points (3%). Charges at this level create quite a drag on your investment performance, which means it can take an exceptionally great year in the stock market to increase your income base. My advice? Stick with GLWB products whose total charges are below 200 basis points (2% of your income base).

So now that we've covered the basics, the question you've got to ask yourself is this: Are GLWB products a good way to generate a retirement income that's guaranteed for the rest of your life and will give you some upside potential if the stock market does well? The following example should help you answer this question.

How a GLWB product might work in retirement

Even though GLWB products appear to provide the potential for upside growth in your retirement income if your investments do well, I wouldn't count on it. To understand why I say this, you'll need to understand the impact of the guarantee fees on your investment and the mechanism of adjusting the maximum withdrawal amount.

Let's first take a look at how your retirement paycheck might be adjusted after you start withdrawing income. For the purposes of this example, we're going to assume you're married and that you and your spouse are both 65 years old. Now let's suppose your income base is $100,000 when you start your retirement paycheck and that you're invested in Prudential's IncomeFlex product. Let's also suppose that you've locked in a maximum withdrawal percentage of 4.5%, as shown in Table 16.1. That means the most you can withdraw in the first year of retirement is $4,500 (that's 4.5% applied to your income base of $100,000). This amount, along with the charges for investment management and insurance guarantees, would be deducted from your income base.

Now let's suppose that the total charges for your investment management expenses plus the insurance guarantee are 159 basis points, or 1.59%, as described previously. In this case, that means that an additional $1,590 would also be deducted from your income base.

Before adding back your investment earnings, your income base by the end of the first year of your retirement would be $93,910 (that's $100,000 - $4,500 - $1,590). For your income base to increase by the end of the first year, your investment earnings would need to exceed $6,090 by year-end in order to get your investment base to $100,000 again. That's a rate of return of a little more than 6% just to break even. If your investments earn less than this amount, your new income base won't be higher than your previous income base and you won't get an increase in your retirement paycheck.

But suppose you earn a rate of return of 7%. In that case, your income base at year-end would be about $101,000 (I've simplified this example, since the actual crediting of investment earnings and account values is more complicated than just adding back in a percentage of funds). If you apply your maximum withdrawal rate of 4.5% to this new income base, your annual maximum guaranteed withdrawal amount is now $4,545 per year, an increase of about 1% over the initial amount of $4,500.

Let's look at that again: To achieve just a 1% increase in your retirement income, your investments would need to earn about 7% in a year. And while it's possible to earn 7% with a portfolio balanced between stocks and bonds, it would be difficult to consistently earn much more than 7% over the course of many years.

Not only that, but if you experience investment losses instead of investment gains, you've dug an investment hole that's hard to get out of. Here's why: Suppose in the first year of retirement, you lose 6% instead of gaining 6%. In this case, that means your income base is now $6,000 less than when you started. Your total year-end income base would then be about $87,910 ($100,000 - $4,500 - $1,590 - $6,000). Now you're down by $12,090, and future investment gains will need to make up all of this loss – plus more – for you to have a chance to experience an increase in your income base. To do that, your investments would need to earn a rate of return of more than 13% in the following year. Possible? Yes, but it's certainly a long shot.

Do GLWBs add value in your retirement years?

They can, if the situation is right, so let's summarize what we've covered about GLWBs so far and look at some shopping tips for those of you interested in GLWB products.

First up, let me address the question most readers are probably curious about: Do GLWB products offer the best of both worlds – systematic withdrawals and immediate annuities – when it comes to generating retirement income?

Unfortunately, "best" is a relative term, and there's no one right answer for everyone. The answer will depend on your goals and the amount of retirement income you need. Although GLWB products offer features of both immediate fixed annuities and systematic withdrawals, they provide an initial amount of retirement income that falls somewhere between the income provided by either method of generating retirement income.

To get a better look at what I mean, Figure 16.2 compares the initial retirement income a couple both age 65 could generate with a GLWB product to what they'd earn from both systematic withdrawals and fixed and inflation-adjusted annuities, using income amounts based on investment information from July 2012.

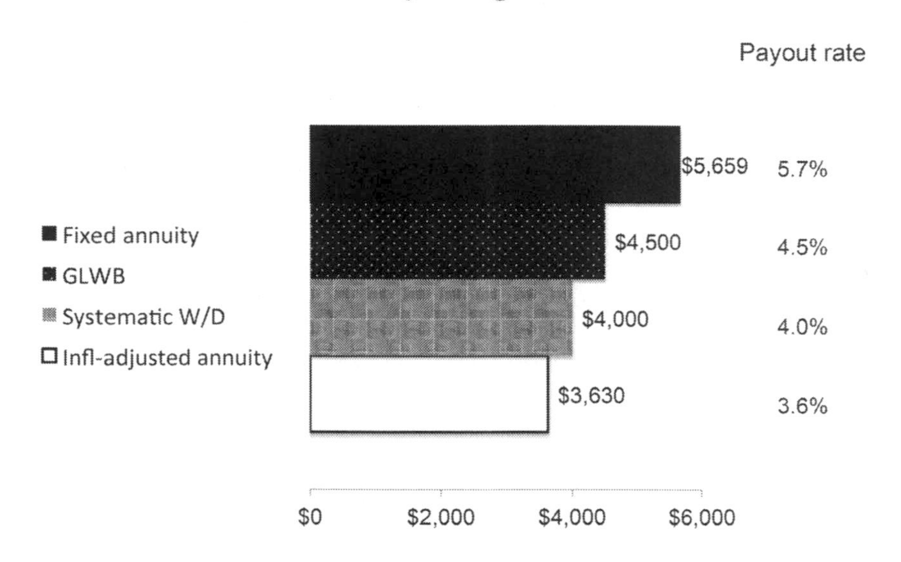

FIGURE 16.2 RETIREMENT INCOME SCORECARD: GLWB COMPARED TO OTHER RIGS

As I've discussed previously, GLWB products have the potential for increasing your retirement income if your investments perform well, but it would take consistently high rates of return to generate meaningful increases in your retirement income. If you need a generous retirement income, you'll most likely realize higher total retirement income over your lifetime with fixed or inflation-adjusted immediate annuities. But remember, with these types of annuities, you can't access your savings once you start the annuity. You also can't leave a monetary legacy to your children or charities, even if you die soon after your retirement income starts, because the company from whom you purchased the annuity gets to keep any remaining funds in your account after you die, no matter when you die.

Systematic withdrawals, on the other hand, will most likely give you more flexible access to your savings and a higher legacy value when you die, compared to

GLWB products. The downside with this investment vehicle is that it doesn't offer a guaranteed lifetime retirement income that won't decrease due to a market downturn.

The experts seem to back up what I have to say about GLWBs. For example, Wade Pfau, PhD maintains an excellent blog on retirement income issues. He published a post in December 2011 titled "GLWBs: Retiree Protection or Money Illusion?" in which he offered an analysis that compared Vanguard's GLWB product to systematic withdrawals. Dr. Pfau concluded that it's very likely that systematic withdrawals would produce a higher retirement paycheck and higher legacy values than a GLWB product would. He also stated that it's possible that purchasing a fixed immediate annuity might enable you to buy a guaranteed income source more cheaply than a GLWB product. If you're interested in reading his article, do an Internet search on the title to find it.

When you compare retirement income-generating methods feature by feature, GLWB products most likely won't come out on top for any specific feature. But they might come in second place for most features, while other methods can rank first in some features but last in others. For some people, GLWB's second-place rankings in many categories might be a desirable outcome.

One important advantage that GLWB products offer is that they address the significant behavioral challenges that people sometimes have regarding generating retirement income. For example, if you like the guarantee of a lifetime retirement income but don't like traditional immediate annuities because you have to give up access to your assets, a GLWB product is the next best thing. Similarly, if you want to use systematic withdrawals so you have access to your savings and because you can invest in the stock market for the potential of growth in your retirement savings and income – but you're scared by the possibility of market crashes – then a GLWB product might also be the next best thing.

I believe that the guarantees offered by GLWB products can be of value to people who want to protect their savings when they're close to retirement as well as generate lifetime income during retirement. But invest in them with the idea that you'll stay with them throughout your entire retirement and won't withdraw all your savings at any point.

Remember, the guarantees of most GLWB products don't apply to any money you withdraw before your retirement starts. So if you withdraw all your money from a GLWB product before you retire because you've changed your mind, you'll have wasted the guarantee fees you paid over the years. And after you start your retirement income, if you withdraw more than the amount specified in the contract, you'll also lose the insurance guarantee (and again will have wasted all those guarantee fees).

If you have any interest in a GLWB product, please take the time to learn everything you can about GLWB products' features and how they compare to other methods of generating retirement income. It could be that other forms of generating retirement income might also meet your needs, or that you could also get the best of both worlds by combining systematic withdrawals with traditional immediate annuities.

GLWB shopping tips

After doing your homework, if you think a GLWB product might best fit your circumstances, here are some shopping tips to help you choose wisely:

- Make sure that the total charges for investment management fees, insurance guarantees, and any other charges don't exceed 200 basis points (2%) of your income base. When you can get GLWB products with fees that are less than this amount from Prudential, Vanguard, and other insurance companies, why pay more? High expense charges will only reduce your retirement income. There are competitively priced GLWB products out there – and products with charges that are just too high. Take the time to learn the difference – it's a good use of your time.

- Don't buy a retail GLWB product that pays a commission to an insurance agent. If someone is pitching you a GLWB product, ask point-blank if there's a commission. These charges will reduce your retirement savings, and there are other GLWB products out there that don't charge a commission.

- Investigate whether the financial institution can increase the charge for insurance. Prudential and Vanguard both offer GLWB products that allow the insurance company to increase this charge up to 1.5% and 2% respectively. This potential action makes me nervous, but it's a fact of life with most GLWB products. I would advise not signing up for any policy that can increase the insurance charge to more than 2%.

When you've found a specific GLWB product you're interested in, I strongly encourage you to take the time to understand how its various features work. Don't invest in anything you don't understand! Most GLWB products offered in 401(k) plans have noncommissioned representatives who can answer any questions you might have.

One last word of advice: As with other annuities, I would suggest not investing all your retirement savings in a GLWB product. It's prudent to diversify your sources of retirement income.

FINAL THOUGHTS

If you've reached this point – congratulations! You've finished the book and fine-tuned your understanding of the tax, investment, insurance, and actuarial issues. You're well on your way to secure your retirement paycheck.

I hope that this book gives you the tools and insights to make the best use of your financial resources and pursue your retirement planning with confidence. Here's to your *rest-of-life*!

• • • • •

Resource List

Here are books, periodicals, and websites that I've found to be helpful for retirement planning.

Books

- *The Blue Zones: Lessons for Living Longer From the People Who've Lived the Longest,* by Dan Buettner, National Geographic 2010.
- *Common Sense on Mutual Funds,* by John Bogle and David Swensen, Wiley 2009.
- *The Hard Times Guide to Retirement Security,* by Mark Miller, Bloomberg Press 2010.
- *Healthy at 100: The Scientifically Proven Secrets of the World's Healthiest and Longest Lived Peoples,* by John Robbins, Ballantine Books 2007.
- *How a Second Grader Beats Wall Street: Golden Rules Any Investor Can Learn,* by Allan Roth, Wiley 2011.
- *Investment Mistakes Even Smart Investors Make, and How to Avoid Them,* by Larry Swedroe, McGraw-Hill 2011.
- *The Mature Mind: The Positive Power of the Aging Brain,* by Gene Cohen, Basic Books 2006.
- *Recession-Proof Your Retirement Years,* by Steve Vernon, *Rest-of-Life* Communications 2010.
- *Social Security for Dummies,* by Jonathan Peterson, For Dummies 2012.
- *Social Security: The Inside Story,* by Andy Landis, CreateSpace 2012.

- *The Ultimate Dividend Playbook: Income, Insight and Independence for Today's Investor,* by Josh Peters, Morningstar 2008.
- *What Color is Your Parachute – For Retirement,* by John Nelson and Richard Bolles, Ten Speed Press 2010.
- *Worth It … Not Worth It? Simple and Profitable Answers to Life's Tough Financial Questions,* by Jack Otter, Business Plus 2012.
- *Your Money or Your Life,* by Vicki Robin, Joe Dominquez, and Monique Tilford, Penguin Books 2008.

Periodicals

- *Retirement Weekly,* edited by Robert Powell, published by MarketWatch

Websites

- *AgeBander* includes a paper by Dr. Somnath Basu and a calculator on the age banding, or bucket, approach to investing and drawing down retirement savings. www.agebander.com
- *The Blue Zones* is a life expectancy calculator customized to your circumstances. www.bluezones.com
- *Bogleheads* includes investment and retirement planning advice inspired by the example of Jack Bogle. www.bogleheads.org
- *CBS MoneyWatch* includes blogs of more than 30 writers on investing, retirement, careers, and consumer finance. www.cbsnews.com/moneywatch
- *Fidelity Retirement Income Planner* includes a tool for estimating retirement living expenses and projecting retirement income from all sources. http://personal.fidelity.com/planning/retirement/income_planner.shtml
- *FIRECalc: A different kind of retirement calculator* includes a calculator using a historical method for determining withdrawal rates. www.firecalc.com
- *HealthView Services* helps you estimate medical expenses in retirement with an online calculator. www.hvsfinancial.com
- *How Much Can I Afford to Spend in Retirement* is a deterministic calculator for determining withdrawal rates using systematic withdrawals, by Ken Steiner. http://howmuchcanIaffordtospendinretirement.webs.com
- *Income Solutions* is an online bidding service for immediate annuities. www.incomesolutions.com

- *Joe Tomlinson blog,* an independent voice and advocate for investment clients, includes articles on developing retirement income. www.josephtomlinson.com
- *Living to 100* is a life expectancy calculator taking into account your family history and lifestyle. www.livingto100.com
- *Money for Life* by Steve Vernon. This free, online retirement planning tutorial organizes more than 150 articles on a variety of retirement planning topics. www.moneyforlifeguideonline.com
- *Morningstar* includes ratings of mutual funds and retirement planning calculators. www.morningstar.com
- *Retirement Researcher Blog* by Dr. Wade Pfau offers independent, data-driven, and research-based information about retirement planning. www.wpfau.blogspot.com
- *Retirement Resource Center,* sponsored by the International Retirement Resource Center, contains a variety of articles and tutorials on retirement planning. www.retirement-resource-center.com
- *RetirementRevised,* developed by Mark Miller, includes articles on career, health, money, and retirement planning. http://retirementrevised.com
- *Simple Life Expectancy Calculator* is from the Society of Actuaries. www.soa.org/research/software-tools/research-simple-life-calculator.aspx
- *Social Security Administration* includes rules on Social Security benefits and an online calculator to estimate Social Security income. www.ssa.gov
- *Social Security Choices* describes strategies that help you maximize your Social Security payout and includes a calculator. www.socialsecuritychoices.com
- *Social Security Timing* also describes strategies that help you maximize your Social Security payout and includes a calculator. www.socialsecuritytiming.com
- *Society of Actuaries* offers a series of 11 briefs on managing retirement decisions. www.soa.org/managing-retirement/
- *T. Rowe Price Retirement Income Calculator* includes a Monte Carlo calculator for determining sustainable withdrawal rates. https://www3.troweprice.com/ric/ricweb/public/ric.do
- *WISER: Women's Institute for a Secure Retirement* includes blogs, calculators, and articles of particular interest to retirement planning for women. www.wiserwomen.org

• • • • •

Acknowledgments

I'd like to thank many people who contributed their time and effort to substantially improve this book.

First, I owe a debt of gratitude to my wife, Melinda, who read the manuscript numerous times and spent countless hours discussing the issues I wanted to cover. She also served as my publishing consultant, commented from a layperson's perspective, and provided encouragement for me to keep plugging away.

Teresa Ciulla is my talented editor. She made the book much easier to read.

Dave Hoak, Jim Isbell, Neil Lloyd, Bev Orth, and Dr. Wade Pfau provided reviews on investment, actuarial, financial, and tax issues. Their comments significantly helped fine-tune the technical descriptions I included in this book.

My interviews with Toni Brown, Francois Gadenne, Bob Powell, Allan Roth, and Larry Swedroe gave me great insights and ideas.

Jack Luff, a research actuary with the Society of Actuaries, provided the latest figures on life expectancies.

I'd also like to thank a number of actuaries and financial professionals with whom I've had many interactions that have deepened my understanding of the issues involved with financing a secure retirement. These helpful individuals include Noel Abkemeier, Don Fuerst, Kelli Hueler, Betty Meredith, Andy Peterson, Anna Rappaport, Steve Siegel, and Joe Tomlinson.

In addition, I'd like to thank several individuals at various financial institutions for sharing details of their retirement income solutions, including Kevin O'Fee and Mike Shamrell at Fidelity Investments, Chris Jones and Katie Solan of Financial Engines, Kelli Hueler at Income Solutions, Sri Reddy of Prudential, Louis Finney and Holly Hollub at UBS, and John Ameriks at Vanguard.

Dinah Berland reviewed the book from the perspective of the target audience. I'm grateful for her suggestions, which helped improve the reader's experience.

Lisa Winger did a great job with the cover design, illustrations, and text layout.

Many other friends also contributed their thoughts and provided encouragement, and I'm grateful for their help. A number of my former colleagues from Watson Wyatt and my clients performed a valuable service as my "focus group" for the cover. Our kids and their spouses – Jeff, Mary Kathryn, Emily, Bonnie, and Spencer – all provided input and helped keep me motivated.

Money for Life wouldn't have been published without all of this help, so I'm very grateful to be part of such a wonderful community.

Index

About the Author

• • • • •

Steve Vernon, F.S.A., has helped Fortune 1000 employers design and manage their retirement programs for more than 35 years. During that time, he worked on the front lines of the extraordinary shift that's taken place in retirement plans, as companies moved from traditional, defined benefit pension plans to 401(k) and other defined contribution plans. This significant change places a tremendous responsibility on individuals to generate a retirement income that lasts for life.

Steve currently writes a regular blog column for CBS MoneyWatch titled "Money for Life," where he addresses the critical topics facing people in retirement. His previously published works include:

- *Money for Life,* a free online retirement planning guide
- *Recession-Proof Your Retirement Years: Simple Retirement Planning Strategies That Work Through Thick or Thin, Rest-of-Life* Communications 2010
- *The Quest: For Long Life, Health and Prosperity* (a DVD/workbook set), *Rest-of-Life* Communications 2007
- *Live Long & Prosper! Invest in Your Happiness, Health and Wealth for Retirement and Beyond,* Wiley 2005
- *Don't Work Forever! Simple Steps Baby Boomers Must Take To Ever Retire,* Wiley 1995

As president of *Rest-of-Life* Communications, Steve delivers retirement planning workshops and conducts retirement education campaigns. He has never sold insurance, annuities, or investments; this enables him to be unbiased in his writing and recommendations.

Steve is a member of the executive faculty and a research fellow with the California Institute for Finance at California Lutheran University, where he conducts research on behavioral finance. In addition, he is a member of the Institutional Retirement Income Council, and he volunteers for a number of research committees for the Society of Actuaries. He also provides consulting to Mercer's U.S. Retirement, Risk and Finance business, focusing on strategic retirement consulting and intellectual capital development. In 2006, he retired as a vice president from Watson Wyatt after a 25-year career.

A Fellow in the Society of Actuaries, Steve graduated summa cum laude from the University of California, Irvine, with a double major in mathematics and social science.

Steve lives in Oxnard, California, with his wife, Melinda, where they're following the advice in this book for their own retirement and *rest-of-life*. For more information, visit www.restoflife.com or email Steve at steve.vernon@restoflife.com.